SIMON PETER

FISHERMAN FROM GALILEE

Books by Ivor Powell

Bible Cameos
Bible Gems
Bible Highways
Bible Names of Christ
Bible Nuggets
Bible Oases
Bible Pinnacles
Bible Promises
Bible Windows
Matthew's Majestic Gospel
Mark's Superb Gospel
Luke's Thrilling Gospel
John's Wonderful Gospel
The Amazing Acts
David: His Life and Times
The Exciting Epistle to the Ephesians
Honey from the Rock
Manna from Heaven
Simon Peter: Fisherman from Galilee
What in the World Will Happen Next?

SIMON PETER

FISHERMAN FROM GALILEE

IVOR POWELL

kregel
PUBLICATIONS

Grand Rapids, MI 49501

Simon Peter: Fisherman from Galilee

Copyright © 1996 by Ivor Powell

Published by Kregel Publications, a division of Kregel, Inc., P.O. Box 2607, Grand Rapids, MI 49501. Kregel Publications provides trusted, biblical publications for Christian growth and service. Your comments and suggestions are valued.

Cover design: Alan G. Hartman
Book design: Nicholas G. Richardson

Library of Congress Cataloging-in-Publication Data
Powell, Ivor, 1910–
    Simon Peter: fisherman from Galilee / Ivor Powell
        p.   cm.
    Includes bibliographical references and index.
    1. Peter, the Apostle, Saint. 2. Apostles—Biography.
I. Title.
BS2515.P68   1996   225.9'2—dc20   96-30471
                                                                                    CIP

ISBN 0-8254-3548-x

Printed in the United States of America
1 2 3 4 5 / 00 99 98 97 96

CONTENTS

PREFACE

Simon Peter, the fisherman from Galilee, was the most exciting of the twelve apostles. It was impossible to predict what he
would do next. He could step out of a fishing boat to walk on the
sea, or get into hotter water denying the Lord at the enemies' fire. He
could be confused wondering if his Master paid taxes, or be inspired
as he exclaimed: "Thou art the Christ, the Son of the living God."
Peter could be outrageously sullen, or completely inspired preaching
to thousands of people. The man could be scared by a servant girl, or
defy a king. Peter made many mistakes, but that possibly accounts
for his popularity. John, who leaned upon the bosom of Christ, in-
spires all people but leaves them with a sense of inferiority, believing they can never be as good as he. Peter relates to everybody, for
in spite of errors, he remained at the forefront of the Lord's work.

When Christians fail temporarily in their assignments, they remember Simon and believe that if he could succeed, so can they.

This volume, which will probably be the last I shall produce, tells
all that I know about this remarkable apostle. He was a man of action
who displayed the characteristics of an evangelist even before he
became one. More than seventy years ago, Peter's example compelled me to follow in his footsteps. Through many countries of the
world I have preached as did he, and now, at the end of my pilgrim-
age, I can say as did Peter, "He is precious." It is fitting that all I
have learned about this great man should be written in this book
which I trust will help all who preach the glorious Gospel of the
Grace of God.

My wife, who has accompanied me on my evangelistic itineraries,
has edited my manuscript, and together we launch this volume on its
world-wide journey.

I am grateful to Kregel Publications of Grand Rapids, Michigan,
for the magnificent way in which they have handled my writings.
There are many wonderful publishers doing the Lord's work, but in

my estimation Kregel Publications will always be among the leaders. I shall always be grateful to Robert Kregel and his son, Jim, for the unceasing assistance given to me.

IVOR POWELL

1

WHY SIMON PETER LEFT BETHSAIDA TO RESIDE IN CAPERNAUM

Matthew, the earliest historian of the church, quoted the words of the Lord when he wrote: "And Jesus answered and said unto him: Blessed art thou, Simon-Barjona, for flesh and blood hath not revealed it unto thee, but my Father which is in heaven" (Matthew 16:17). John said that Philip was from Bethsaida, the city of Andrew and Peter (John 1:44). Probably, the man later called "the Big Fisherman," was born in Bethsaida and continued to live there during his adolescence. Why he decided to reside in Capernaum was never explained.

Bethsaida was a small village close to the northern shore of the Sea of Galilee. Most of its inhabitants were employed in the fishing industry, but since the river Jordan supplied plenty of water, agriculture was also important within the community. Boats were made and repaired; fishing nets were also produced, and many side industries connected with fishing flourished in the area. More difficult tasks were transferred to the larger city Capernaum, which was only a few miles away. It may seem surprising that although Simon Peter became known as a citizen of Capernaum, he remained identified with his former place of residence. John referred to him as a man from Bethsaida. This seems to support the conclusion that approaching manhood, he decided to seek his fortune in a new locality. To consider why this decision was made, the following suggestions are offered.

1. Did Jonas, the head of the family, decide to move to the larger city? Did his family accompany him?

There was a government-controlled tax office in Capernaum, and all the caravan routes passed through the thriving center. The desert highways brought many travelers to the city, and after journeying for weeks through barren terrain, people would be enthusiastic about buying fish and enjoying a change of diet. Financial resources would need to be considerable, for at least two sons, Andrew and Simon, would soon desire to start their own business. If they were to be assisted, prosperity was essential. It seems feasible that the family moved to Capernaum because the larger city offered greater opportunities for success. Perhaps their fishing boats were already anchored in the harbor, and it only remained to establish a home and meet new neighbors.

2. Did Simon and Andrew wish to become independent?

That they were in partnership with Zebedee suggests the arrangement was mutually satisfactory to both families. At first Simon and Andrew may have been employed by their friend who saw in the two hard-working boys the opportunity to extend his business. Eventually they may have been accepted as junior partners. Probably, there were many other fishing boats which worked out of the harbor, and competition could have been great. When repairs had to be done on boats or nets, it would have been advantageous for the young men to take advantage of local facilities. To live close to the shipyards where work could be observed offered great advantages. If the people of Capernaum had anything like newspapers, the growth of the new firm would have been front-page news.

3. Did the young woman whom Simon married influence her husband's decision?

It is known that Simon's mother-in-law resided in Capernaum. She was the lady whom Jesus healed after a service in the nearby synagogue (see Luke 4:38–39). It is not known how, where, or when Simon first met his wife-to-be, but it was not a cause for amazement when the couple decided to live with the parent. Nothing was ever written about the wife's father; maybe he had died. If the mother and daughter had lived alone, it would be wise for the newlyweds to remain, at least for a while, in the home of the bride. Even today many young people follow that example until they become independent by either buying or renting an apartment.

Archaeologists believe they have found the remains of the home where Simon and his wife lived, and if their findings be correct, it can be asserted that the house was within a stone's throw of the local synagogue. There could have been other reasons the decision was made to move to Capernaum, but at least these suggestions might explain why this family went to live in the more prosperous city. Simon could have become a prominent citizen of the community; he spoke his mind, and exercised considerable influence over people, and was a leader of men. Not much is known about his religious convictions but there is reason to believe that like others of his time, he attended the synagogue and obeyed the commandments taught by the rabbi. Had not Jesus of Nazareth changed his life, Simon might have become one of the most influential citizens of his community. It is not known whether Andrew lived in his own apartment, or if Simon's home was sufficiently large to accommodate him.

2

SIMON PETER'S
FIRST MEETING WITH JESUS

Matthew wrote: "And Jesus, walking by the sea of Galilee, saw two brethren, Simon called Peter, and Andrew his brother, casting a net into the sea. *For they were fishers*" (Matthew 4:18). The men were partners with James and John in the fishing industry; their work was never easy; the occupation created many problems; the work was exceptionally demanding. When the men were ashore, boats needed to be overhauled, and the nets maintained. The fact that Simon's brother became one of the disciples of John the Baptist could have produced tension between the two men (see John 1:35 and 40). The appearance of the preacher sent shock waves through the religious community, and great crowds hastened to attend his meetings.

The Jordan Valley became a scene of unending activity, and many people listened attentively to the evangelist's message. Some men scoffed, others became interested. Some young men decided to remain with the preacher, and soon John had a group of disciples who were devoted to their master.

Peter's Concern . . . *How Understandable*

As the excitement spread through Galilee, many people temporarily left their occupation in order to hear the man who had captured the attention of the entire population. Many soon returned to their homes, but a few remained. The power of John the Baptist could not be denied, and several of the listeners became devoted followers. The Greek word translated "disciple" was *mathetés*—which meant *a student* or *pupil*. Andrew became interested and Simon was hardly surprised when his brother expressed a desire to hear the man about whom everybody was talking. John was conducting his services in the Jordan Valley, and since this was only a short distance away, it was not difficult for Andrew to join the crowds converging on the meeting place. Simon had no objection, but when Andrew extended his visit and failed to return, the situation became alarming. He was needed, for Simon could not handle their business alone. Where in the world was Andrew? Simon waited in vain for his brother, and probably became irritable when he failed to appear. Peter would have sympathized with Martha of Bethany who complained of a similar experience. When she was overwhelmed by kitchen duties, she looked for assistance from her sister, Mary, who seemed oblivious of the need to provide a meal for their visitors (see Luke 10:39–40). It is not known how long Andrew stayed away from his work, but it is safe to assume the longer he remained with John, the more disturbed became his impatient brother.

Peter's Curiosity ... *How Uncontrollable*

When eventually Andrew returned, his face was flushed with excitement and his speech animated. Many years later John remembered that occasion and wrote: "He [Andrew] first findeth his own brother Simon, and saith unto him, We have found the Messiah, which is being interpreted the Christ. And he brought him to Jesus" (see John 1:40–41). The irate brother might have asked: "Where have you been? Why did you stay away so long? Are you out of your mind? What about our fishing? If we cannot supply our customers, we may lose their business." Probably Andrew never heard a word of the complaint; he was anxious to share his faith. Even Simon Peter became curious to know what had happened. Andrew was so desirous to share his happiness, he left the Savior in order to persuade his brother to see for himself the charm of the Messiah.

As Simon listened to Andrew's testimony, his anger began to disappear; he was fascinated by what he was seeing and hearing. His subdued brother had been changed. When he grabbed Peter's arm and said, "Come and see for yourself," his curiosity became overwhelming and, possibly shaking his head, he allowed himself to be led away from the fishing boats. He had to see for himself what was happening at the Jordan River. Andrew's eyes were shining; he was becoming proficient at winning people for his new Master. (See Homily No. 1 at the conclusion of this chapter.)

Peter's Confrontation ... *How Unforgettable*

"And when Jesus beheld him, he said: Thou art Simon the son of Jonas. Thou shalt be called Cephas, which is by interpretation, A stone" (John 1:42).

15

The Lord was very deliberate; He spoke as if He had known Simon for many years, and the fisherman seemed to be speechless. Nothing more was said, and ultimately Simon returned to Capernaum. To use the language of the fishing community—Peter had been hooked, but Jesus permitted his catch to run! Simon was not asked to follow the Lord; and apparently did not receive any other invitation. Perhaps he was disappointed, for it seemed the new Prophet was independent. Nevertheless, Peter was unable to forget the eyes of Jesus which seemed to be pools of compassion. If he tried to forget his encounter with the Savior, he failed. He was an expert at extracting hooks from the fish, but was unable to remove the other kind of hook embedded within his soul.

I shall never forget the first time I went fishing for salmon. I knew nothing about the art, but a minister friend was determined to teach me. He baited the hook, ran out the line and told me to take a seat in the back of his boat. I do not think I really caught the fish; maybe it decided to commit suicide. When the tip of my rod suddenly dipped, my friend yelled "Let him go, let him go." I could do nothing else, for that fish was trying to break the speed limit as it made for the open sea! When it paused to rest, my friend said: "Now reel him in." The captive was too tired to resist, and eventually I lifted the fish into the boat. I am sure the Lord permitted Peter's return to Capernaum because the man had been securely hooked! Jesus knew how to catch men. When Simon returned to his own boat, he was unable to forget the gleam he had seen in the eyes of the Lord. That initial meeting with the Son of God became very productive.

HOMILY NO. 1

Andrew ... *The Patron Saint of Personal Workers*

Andrew was a go-getter; and if some readers are unfamiliar with this questionable terminology, an explanation will be welcome. A go-getter is a man who stops at nothing. In order to attain his ends he will remove mountains, cross oceans, turn the world inside out, laugh at impossibilities, and finally set a city on fire while other people are looking for a match! A go-getter is a man who goes and gets what he desires, and woe betide anyone who stands in the way. Failure is never admitted, for the untiring man continues until his purpose is fully achieved. Andrew was a man of this caliber. He knew what he wanted and always took the short cut to reach it. Other men became the great generals in the holy war; but Andrew planned the campaigns, removed the difficulties, and prepared the way for every fresh advance. He was a great go-getter, the patron saint of all who seek souls for Christ.

Andrew First Found Peter

Jesus of Nazareth had been entertaining guests, and one of the privileged visitors was Andrew. He had been standing with John the Baptist when the Stranger passed, and hearing John say, "Behold the Lamb of God," Andrew and another disciple had followed Christ. When they received the invitation to accompany the Savior, they gladly accepted the hospitality of the new Friend, and stayed with Him the rest of the day. "And one of them which heard John speak . . . was Andrew, Simon Peter's brother. He first findeth his own brother Simon, and saith unto him, We have found the Messiah . . . And he brought him to Jesus." There was no fuss about this quiet man. He had been with Jesus and was fully assured that his findings were correct. *We have found the Messiah*" echoed the certainty of his soul, and that was that! Until this time Andrew took pride of place from his brother Simon. It is interesting to notice that the sacred record says of Bethsaida, "It was the city of Andrew and Peter" (John 1:44). Perhaps Andrew was the elder brother.

Andrew First Found the Lad with the Loaves

When the Lord had gathered together His band of disciples, He separated them into couples in order that their ministry might become more effective. And in the new arrangement it would appear that Andrew's partner was Philip, for their names are not only coupled together in the official list (Mark 3:18), but these men are seen together on later occasions. "When Jesus saw a great company come unto him, he saith unto Philip, Whence shall we buy bread that these may eat? . . . Philip answered him, Two hundred penny worth of bread is not sufficient for them, that every one of them may take a little. One of his disciples, Andrew, Simon Peter's brother, saith unto him, There is a lad which hath five barley loaves, and two small fishes: but what are they among so many?" (John 6:5–9). Were his eyes alight with expectation as he uttered those words? The provisions were so inadequate that to mention them on such an occasion was an act of stupidity—unless Andrew had very strong reasons for so doing. While the other disciples were regretting their inability to feed the crowd, Andrew was investigating the position. He discovered a boy's lunch. The big man and the small boy pooled their resources, and through them the Master fed a multitude.

Andrew First Brought the Gentiles to Jesus

"And there were certain Greeks among them that came up to worship at the feast: The same came therefore to Philip which was of Bethsaida of Galilee, and desired him, saying, Sir, we would see Jesus. Philip cometh and telleth Andrew: and again Andrew and Philip tell Jesus" (John 12:20–22).

"Philip was puzzled. Let us not blame him, for this marked a new departure in the affairs of discipleship. These Greeks were proselytes, but they were still Gentiles. Had they any part in Messianic privileges? Would their inclusion result in troublesome repercussions? 'Andrew, what do you think about it?' And when Andrew had shrewdly considered the matter, he replied, 'Philip, we'll tell the Master. He'll know what to do.' 'And Andrew and Philip tell Jesus.' And Jesus answered, 'The hour is come that the Son of man should be glorified. . . . And I, if I be lifted up from the earth, will draw all men unto me.' Andrew reminded the Lord of the great world of seeking Gentiles: the Lord gave to Andrew the privilege of bringing those Gentiles to Him. And, perhaps, that is the reason why this disciple became the patron saint of all personal workers for Christ." (Reprinted from the author's commentary, *John's Wonderful Gospel*, Kregel Publications, Grand Rapids, Michigan.)

3

THREE CONFLICTING ACCOUNTS, AN INTERRUPTED SERVICE, AND A THOUGHTLESS INVITATION

I f it were possible, I would like to speak with Matthew, Mark and Luke to ask why their accounts are different in the synoptic Gospels. For example, Matthew described how the Lord walked along the seashore to call Simon Peter, Andrew, James and John into full-time discipleship (Matthew 4:18). Much later (Matthew 8:14), we are informed that Christ entered into the home of Simon Peter to restore a sick mother-in-law.

Mark appears to have a different version. He states the Savior first called His disciples and then entered immediately into the synagogue. Afterward the miracle was performed (Mark 1:29). Luke supplied another explanation. He described how Jesus attended the service in the synagogues, and then went into the home of Simon. The next morning (or later), He went to the beach and invited the fishermen to become disciples. These conflicting accounts explain why I would like to speak with the three writers; to ask questions and receive answers and solve my problems.

It must be remembered that none of the three men had been eyewitnesses of the events. Matthew had not yet met the Savior, Mark was a youth in Jerusalem, and Luke was in a distant country. He did not enter the story until he became an associate of Paul the first missionary. Matthew possibly obtained his information from another disciple; Mark, who became the amanuensis of Peter, probably heard the account from his mentor; Luke heard it first either from Paul, or one of the disciples. The writers of the Gospels could only express what they were told by an informant. It is impossible to be authoritative about the chronological order of the events, but some details appear to be convincing. Matthew and Mark were content to tell what had happened; when the events actually took place was of little, if any, consequence. Everybody appears to agree that Jesus went into the synagogue *on the sabbath day* when work of any kind was forbidden. The day of rest began and ended with sunset; work on fishing nets would not be permitted either before or after the religious services. Luke, the beloved physician of the early church, was accustomed to writing notes, and methodical in preserving records. Some might suggest the men went to the beach immediately after they left the synagogue, but that would be unlikely since the fishermen accompanied the Lord into the home of Simon.

It must be remembered that when the Lord emerged from the house, a huge crowd had gathered in the street; they had brought sick relatives hoping Jesus would again display His ability to heal. It was never revealed where the Savior spent the following night; He might have been invited to stay with Peter's family, or He could have climbed into the hills to commune with His Father. The following morning He descended to the shore to call His first disciples. This explanation is not meant to be argumentative. Whether or not these deductions are conclusive is of minor consequence; they at least provide a base from which this study can proceed.

The Service in the Sanctuary ... *Disturbed*

The city of Capernaum was probably bathed in sunlight as worshippers walked toward the synagogue. They came from all directions, but no one anticipated what was to happen. Simon and Andrew had put on their Sabbath clothing, for it was expected that all worshippers should be suitably attired. Unfortunately, Peter's wife had been compelled to remain at home; her mother was sick with a fever. The two men entered the building, went to their customary seats and prepared to listen to the rabbi. Suddenly, one of the brothers nudged his companion and pointed toward the entrance. Jesus of Nazareth, Whom they had met at the river Jordan, was entering the building. They watched as He found a seat, and by that time many in the congregation were aware of the Savior's presence.

"And in the synagogue there was a man which had a spirit of an unclean devil, and cried with a loud voice, saying, Let us alone. What have we to do with thee, thou Jesus of Nazareth? art thou come to destroy us? I know thee who thou art; the Holy One of God. And Jesus rebuked him, saying, Hold thy peace and come out of him. And when the devil had thrown

20

him in the midst, he came out of him, and hurt him not. And they were all amazed, and spake among themselves, saying: What a word is this? for with authority and power, he commandeth the unclean spirits, and they come out" (Luke 4:33–36).

There is reason to believe that all the people in the building knew the man whose raucous voice had echoed through the sanctuary. He appeared to be harmless as he sat quietly in the service. Even if he were unable to understand the rabbi's sermon, he was always quiet and respectful. The listeners were appalled when the afflicted man jumped to his feet and yelled at Jesus. He had desecrated the sanctuary and should be expelled immediately. The Stranger quietly responded saying: "Hold thy peace and come out of him." The man collapsed on the floor, and after his body seemed torn by convulsions, signs of intelligence began to appear on his face. He seemed to be awakening from a terrible nightmare. He was the same person, and yet unmistakably different. The man had been amazingly transformed; sanity shone in his eyes.

There is no evidence to prove the service ever commenced or completed. The cantor was unable to sing, and the rabbi remained silent; the congregation was excited; respect for the house of God had temporarily been forgotten. Simon Peter was spellbound, and within a few minutes, he and his brother were standing in the street. They heard the horrible sounds which seemed to be sinister, suggesting the presence of evil. Perhaps the brothers had been preparing to assist in the man's eviction when suddenly the miracle was performed.

They would never forget how the demoniac began gesturing to people he knew. When the congregation returned to their homes, Simon and Andrew looked at Jesus, Who possibly was standing as if considering what His next move should be. Luke wrote: "And he arose out of the synagogue and entered into the house of Simon" (Luke 4:38).

The Savior and the Sick Woman . . . *How Delightful*

It would be nice to know if Peter invited the Lord to share a meal or if Jesus proceeded directly to the home knowing a sick lady needed assistance. As far as is known the Lord came to Capernaum alone. If that be correct, He might have been standing as if He had nowhere to go. Did the two brothers spontaneously invite Him to dinner? This would be the natural thing to do, especially if they were aware of an increasing yearning within their souls. Perhaps they were thinking of the mother-in-law, and hoping the Lord would heal her. Maybe the Savior did not wait for an invitation and proceeded directly to Peter's home. Yet, the former suggestion appears to be attractive, for the Lord loved to be asked to dine with people.

Jesus became the chief Guest at a banquet arranged by Matthew (Luke 5:29). When Jesus went into the home of Zacchaeus, the Pharisees criticized this action, saying He was gone to be the guest of a man who was a sinner (Luke 19:7). When the two disciples who were returning to Emmaus invited their Companion to supper, the Lord graciously accepted and later "was revealed unto them in the breaking of bread" (Luke 24:30–31).

"And they besought him for her" (Luke 4:38).

If Peter's wife were unaware of the extra guests for dinner she might have been exasperated, but she was aware of her husband's impetuosity. He made hasty decisions and repented at leisure. The fact that Simon and Andrew were accompanied by James, John and Jesus, meant there would be five hungry men to feed and since her mother was indisposed, that overworked wife had no time to spare. Most women would have given their husbands a piece of their mind! She only had one pair of hands! Probably everybody was asked to be seated, and during the ensuing conversation someone mentioned the lady who was confined to her bed. It is interesting to read that "they besought him for her." Luke, the doctor, stated she was ill with a great fever—her need was urgent.

"And he stood over her, and rebuked the fever and it left her, and immediately she arose and ministered unto them" (Luke 4:39).

Many men dislike their mothers-in-law, but Simon had one worth her weight in gold.

HOMILY NO. 2

The Master . . . *Responding*

"The house was very silent; the people were sad; Peter's mother-in-law was gravely ill. Her fever had become progressively worse

22

and there were fears she might die. Already Simon had become acquainted with Jesus, and the news that the travelers were approaching the house increased the hope that the Healer might help the stricken woman. Three things demand attention: (1) *A serious position*. The woman was very sick; she had *a great fever*. Her condition was extremely grave. (2) *A sincere prayer*. "And they besought Him for her." He had hardly entered the homestead when someone told Him their friend was very ill. Could He render assistance? Happy indeed is the person who has interceding friends. (3) *A sublime power*. The Lord Jesus went to the side of the sick woman, and within seconds His mighty power banished the fever. This was an example of other desires existing deep within His heart. He believed the whole world was sick of a great fever; and had come to earth to minister healing to the needy. He loved to be asked to do this. Need should beget faith, and faith should promote prayer. When these prerequisites are forthcoming, anything is possible. *His touch has still its ancient power; no word from Him can fruitless fall.*

The Malady . . . *Restricting*

If Peter's home originally belonged to his wife's mother, the dwelling could have remained her property and she the head of the family. The daughter would be a comfort and help to her mother, who was suffering from a deadly fever. It was significant that Doctor Luke stated she was taken with a great fever—her condition was dangerous. Confined to her bed, she was probably embarrassed to hear about the unexpected guests for dinner—she was unable to help. Her story may be considered under four headings. Her danger; deliverance; duty; and delight.

Danger

It should be remembered the Lord came to her; she neither asked for, nor expected, help from a stranger. When Jesus entered her bedroom, she probably wondered who had come to visit. She was helpless and completely unable to save herself. The woman must have been a very patient soul, for she was willing for temperamental Simon and his more subdued brother to share the home.

Deliverance

Probably she did not know that friends in the other room had already asked the Lord to help. Maybe she had heard from Andrew and Simon about the great Person they had met when attending John's meetings. Within moments she was able to exclaim: "He is MY Savior" and was helping to provide a meal for her new Friend.

Duty

Peter's wife must have been shocked when her mother rushed into the kitchen issuing orders to everybody there. If the younger woman became anxious, that was to be expected. One minute her parent had been gravely ill; the next she was rushing around the kitchen preparing a meal. Most people would have required time for recuperation; the fever might return! This woman never stopped to consider that possibility. If the exertion proved to be fatal, she would die happily serving her Savior.

Delight

There is reason to believe she never forgot that Sabbath day, and her example should be an inspiration for all Christians. That woman would appreciate one of our modern hymns:

> Shackled by a heavy burden
> Neath a load of guilt and shame;
> Then the hand of Jesus touched me,
> And now I am no longer the same.
>
> He touched me, Oh, He touched me
> And Oh, the joy that filled my soul.
> Something happened, and now I know
> He touched me and made me whole.

The Scene at Sunset . . . *How Demanding*

"And at even, when the sun did set, they brought unto him all that were diseased, and them that were possessed with devils, And all the city was gathered together at the door" (Mark 1:32).

The meal was over, the dishes washed, and the fellowship ended. The Lord thanked Peter's wife for her hospitality, but as Peter opened the door everybody stared at a crowd of people filling the street. News had traveled fast, and the story of the miracle in the synagogue had been repeated throughout the city. Hurriedly, families brought their afflicted loved ones and hoping they would be helped, waited expectantly in the streets. When the Savior saw them, compassion filled His soul. Within moments He moved among the sufferers, and His touch answered innumerable prayers. "Many were healed." That section of Capernaum became an open-air cathedral as the power of God transformed people with urgent need. It is worthy of attention that Mark said *many* were healed" (Mark 1:34). Did that infer Christ did not heal everybody; that for reasons unknown some were not helped? Perhaps the writer was expressing the fact that so many were delivered it seemed impossible to count their number. Some might ask how this applies to modern society, and Canan H. Twell supplies the answer. He wrote:

At even ere the sun did set;
The sick, O Lord, around Thee lay
Oh, in what divers pain they met,
Oh, with what joy they went away.

Once more 'tis eventide,
And we oppressed with various ills draw near.
What if Thy form we cannot see?
We know and feel that Thou art here.

O Savior Christ, our woes dispel,
for some are sick, and some are sad.
And some have never loved Thee well,
And some have lost the love they had.

And all O Lord, crave perfect rest
And to be wholly free from sin;
And they who fain would serve Thee best,
Are conscious most of wrong within.

O Savior Christ, Thou too art man,
Thou hast been troubled, tempted, tried;
Thy kind but searching glance can scan
The very wounds that shame would hide.

Thy touch has still its ancient power,
No word from Thee can fruitless fall.
Hear, in this solemn evening hour,
And in Thy mercy heal us all.

The Mother-in-Law ... *Rejoicing*

"The people who were near the bedside were surely astonished, for within moments the fever was obviously dying. When signs of health returned to the face of the sick woman an intense gratitude thrilled her soul. '. . . *and immediately she arose and ministered unto them.*' Once again there are three things which invite our attention: (1) *Her demanding devotion.* As she looked into the face of Jesus, her heart throbbed with wonderful exhilaration. She was now in His debt; He had done for her what no other could have done. She would always be grateful, but that was not enough. Whereas others might have said, 'Lord, I hope that someday I shall have the chance to do something for you,' she recognized something could be done immediately. (2) *Her dedicated deeds.* 'She arose and ministered unto them.' We are not told precisely what other people might have been included in the 'them,' but we may be assured that in serving others she also served Him. Probably she prepared a meal, and the possibility exists that there were other tasks also which she performed on His behalf. When these ladies dedicate their talents to Christ, they are angels in disguise. (3) *Her deepening delight.* When she saw smiles upon His face and noticed how He appreciated the meal, her heart filled with joy. She had been able to do something for her Lord, and this was all the compensation needed for a task well done. Nevertheless, in a deeper sense she had died to self. Some people arising from a sick bed would have found all manner of excuses to avoid going into the kitchen. They would need time to recuperate! They would need to rest lest the symptoms of sickness return. Some people expect a lot of attention even after they get well! This delightful woman gently pushed the people out of her path. Her Lord was hungry; something had to be done about it! Thus any idea of self-gratification was forgotten. Her self-life, if such it may be called, had been absorbed in her increasing love for Jesus. She was dead, and yet she was alive; in another sense she was not living; His life was filling her. It would be very difficult to say who was the happier that day—Peter's wife's mother, or the Lord Jesus" (copied in part from the author's commentary, *Luke's Thrilling Gospel*, Kregel Publications, Grand Rapids, Michigan).

26

4

ONE OF THE FIRST DISCIPLES
CALLED BY THE SAVIOR

"And it came to pass, that, as the people pressed upon him to hear the word of God, he stood by the lake of Gennesaret. And saw two ships standing by the lake; but the fishermen were gone out of them, and were washing their nets" (Luke 5:1–2).

Mention has already been made of the varying accounts in the synoptic Gospels. Here again it becomes evident that either from a lapse of memory or unknown reasons, the writers of the first three Gospels did not agree precisely on the chronological order of events in the early ministry of Jesus. It is interesting to discover that some theologians believe the Lord duplicated His visits to Galilee to allow time for the fishermen to arrange for the disposal of the fishermen's gear. It is suggested that first the Lord "nominated" certain men, but delayed the final call until they had either sold their boats, or arranged for other men to continue the family business (*The Pulpit Commentary*). Whether or not this interpretation has merit is difficult to decide, but for the purpose of this study it is sufficient to accept Luke's account and examine what he presented.

The Service on the Shore

"And he entered into one of the ships, which was Simon's, and prayed him that he would thrust out a little from the land. And he sat down and taught the people out of the ship" (Luke 5:3).

Once again there are conflicting details regarding the time which elapsed between the visit to Simon's house, and the morning when the Lord asked for the use of the fishing boat. Mark states that following the visit to the home in Capernaum, early in the morning the Savior went into a solitary place and was followed by Simon and others who said to Jesus: "All men seek for thee." Mark suggests the service on the shore took place much earlier (compare Mark 1:16–20 with Mark 1:32). Luke states that between the two incidents was a preaching itinerary in which Jesus "preached in the synagogues of Galilee" (Luke 4:44). It is difficult to decide which was the exact morning when the Lord asked for the use of Simon's boat. We must be content to consider the account supplied by Luke.

The men had evidently been at the fishing grounds all night, for Simon said to Jesus: "We have toiled all the night and have taken nothing." Disappointed, tired and frustrated, they had brought their vessels to the shore and were removing debris from the nets. At some point during this procedure, Simon Peter became aware of the approach of a crowd, and recognized the people were following Jesus. When asked for the use of their boat, the fisherman consented and was glad to have an opportunity to repay some of the debt owed to his new Friend. The Lord was asked to take a seat in the back of the fishing boat, and skillfully maneuvering the oars, Simon arranged that Jesus could face the people waiting expectantly on the beach. Apparently there was no request for healing; the listeners were content to listen. The theme of the Savior's message was not revealed, but whatever was spoken, was heard by Simon who sat within a few feet of the Preacher.

Suddenly, when the discourse ended, Jesus turned and said: "Simon, launch out into the deep, and let down your nets for a draught." The Lord desired to compensate the fishermen for their cooperation. It should never be forgotten that God always pays His debts. People who refuse to work for the Savior advertise their stupidity. For each day of dedicated service, God recompenses His servants with happiness; and for every sacrifice made on His behalf, He pays in gold! The great catch of fish more than rewarded the men for anything they had done. Peter and Andrew possessed at least two nets, and this applied also to their partners. When the boats commenced to sink, the incident seemed related to a promise made by the Lord. "Give, and it shall be given unto you; good measure, pressed down, and shaken together, and running over, shall men give into your bosom" (Luke 6:38).

We can only surmise what Peter thought as he listened to the Savior's sermon. The later events which led to his confession of unworthiness, suggested he had become extremely uncomfortable. Although he had been seated behind the Speaker, he felt the words were being addressed directly to him. The astonishment expressed at the huge catch of fish was the outburst of something which had been simmering within his soul. His conviction was deepening but, unfortunately, his faith remained weak.

When the Lord said: "Let down your nets for a draught," Peter replied: "Master, we have toiled all the night and have taken nothing. Nevertheless at thy word, I will let down *the net*" (Luke 5:4–5). Evidently Jesus knew how many fish would be forthcoming, and that *nets* would be necessary to hold the catch. Simon was unable to comprehend this fact, and reluctantly he agreed to use *one net*. Had he paid more attention to the command of Christ, his net would not have been damaged.

The Sinking of the Ships

"And when they had this done, they inclosed a great multitude of fishes, and their net brake. And they beckoned unto their partners which were in the other ship, that they should come and help them, and they came, and filled both the ships, so that they began to sink" (Luke 5:6–7).

Today the Sea of Galilee represents a thriving industry. The government has used spectacular methods to control the fish. It is no longer necessary to seek the shoals; the fishermen know where they are to be found at any time of the day or night. During one of my visits to Israel, I stayed in a motel close to the Sea of Galilee, and was present when men brought ashore their catch. It was truly an unforgettable sight, for the fish were much larger than salmon. I spoke with the fishermen and learned how modern technology had revolutionized their industry. The Department of Fisheries has studied the movement of shoals and know where they may be found at any time. Certain critics deny the accuracy of the Biblical record, but there is no problem in the story. It is not even certain that this occurrence was a miracle. Dr. Tristam in his excellent book, *The Natural History of the Bible*, page 285, says: "The thickness of the shoals of fish in the lake of Gennesaret is almost incredible to anyone who has not witnessed them. They often cover the area of more than an acre, and when the fish move slowly forward in a mass, and are rising out of the water, it appears as though a heavy rain were beating down on the surface of the lake." Dr. W. M. Thompson supplies information concerning the deep sea nets used by fishermen on the Sea of Galilee. He says: "Again, there is the bag-net or basket-net, of various kinds, which are so constructed and worked as to enclose the fish out in deep water. I have seen them of almost every conceivable size and pattern. It was with one of this sort, I suppose, that Simon had toiled all night without catching anything, but which, when let down at the command of Jesus, enclosed so great a multitude that the net broke, and they filled two ships with the fish until they began to sink. Peter here speaks of toiling all night; and there are certain kinds of fishing always carried on at night. It is a beautiful sight. With blazing torch, the boat glides over the flashing sea; and the men stand gazing keenly into it until their prey is sighted, when, quick as lightning, they fling their net or fly their spear; and often you see the tired fishermen come sullenly into harbour in the morning, having toiled all night in vain. Indeed, every kind of fishing is uncertain. A dozen times the angler jerks out a naked hook; the hand-net closes down on nothing; the drag-net brings in only weeds; the bag comes up empty. And then, again, every throw is successful, every net is full—and frequently without any other apparent reason than that of throwing it on the right side of the ship instead of the left, as it happened to the disciples here at Tiberias" (*The Land and the Book*, W. M. Thompson, p. 393, Thomas Nelson and Sons).

When Peter saw the size of his catch of fish he was astonished; but as the ships began to sink he was scared. They were still in deep water and he had no desire to lose the fish, swim to the shore, nor drown. That he succeeded in bringing the catch to land seems evident, but what happened to them, remains uncertain. Some suggestions may be considered.

Probably a large part of the crowd still lingered on the shore; they were hoping to see additional miracles. If they had been following the Lord for a long time, they might have been hungry and ready to cook breakfast! Since the fishermen were about to leave their occupation, the fish could have been sold to customers on the beach. The sudden departure of the wage-earners caused inconvenience to everybody concerned.

It is thought-provoking that Simon and his friends left their boats immediately to become permanent disciples of the Savior. Maybe the "hired servants" mentioned in the Gospel took over the business and managed it for the absent fishermen (see Mark 1:20).

The Savior and the Sinner

"When Simon Peter saw it, he fell down at Jesus' knees, saying, Depart from me for I am a sinful man, O Lord . . . and when they had brought their ships to land, they forsook all, and followed him" (Luke 5:8 and 11).

The Message, the Miracle, and the Man

The Lord said: "Come ye after me, and I will make you to become fishers of men" (Mark 1:17). Apparently there was no message concerning repentance, but it must be remembered that Simon had heard every word uttered by Jesus. He consented to the use of the fishing boat because it was the proper thing to do. The Lord had been very gracious in healing the mother-in-law. The final impression made upon the men was made by the huge catch of fish. Jesus had been aware of the presence and size of the shoal, for He had directed the men to the correct place on the lake, and urged them to let down more than one net. Yet, when Peter saw the amazing catch, he forgot the fish, and became conscious of unworthiness. When he understood the significance of the Lord's invitation, he realized the Lord had not come to call saints and angels, but sinners comparable to fishermen. Peter and the other men were enrolled in God's Academy where Jesus was the Head Teacher. He would correct their mistakes, refine their character, and superintend every phase of their spiritual education until they graduated with honors.

5

THE FIVE STAGES OF
SIMON PETER'S TRAINING

When the disciples of Jesus reminisced, two monumental occasions stood out in bold relief. The first was the call which took them from their fishing boats to become followers of the Savior. The second was the day of their ordination to become ministers of the Gospel. The time between these events was spent in training for their important vocation. It is not known how long this period of tuition lasted, but a comparison of the first three Gospels reveals that certain things took place which helped prepare the men for the arduous tasks ahead.

Matthew states that during this training the Lord performed four miracles; delivered the Sermon on the Mount, stilled a storm on the Sea of Galilee, and called Matthew to become a disciple. Mark says that Jesus called Matthew and performed three miracles. Luke describes three miracles, and cites the call of Matthew. It may be significant that all three of the synoptic writers mentioned the call of Matthew, the healing of the man who suffered from the palsy, and the cleansing of the leper. It is evident that as the disciples associated with their Master, all the events mentioned were woven into the fabric of their spiritual education. If they were to be effective representatives of Jesus, they would need to emulate His example, understand His message, and to the best of their ability, reproduce what was seen in Him.

Leaving . . . *How Compelling*

"And when they had brought their ships to land, they forsook all, and followed him" (Luke 5:11).

At one point in the Lord's ministry, three young men made excuses for their reluctance to become disciples. One said he was willing to follow unconditionally, but he changed his mind when he heard of the Savior having no place to lay His head. The second wished to delay his decision until he buried his father, and the third said he was willing, but thought it wise and proper first to say farewell to his family. The Lord replied: "No man, having put his hand to the plough, and looking back, is fit for the kingdom of God" (see Luke 9:57–62). Simon Peter and his colleagues realized it was necessary to make a choice; they could not become full-time disciples and stay with their fishing boats. One of these callings had to be abandoned in favor of the other.

Looking . . . *How Captivating*

"They forsook all and followed HIM" (Luke 5:11).

Simon quickly discovered the only successful way to be a true disciple was to keep his eyes focused on the Lord. Later in a great impulsive expression of faith, he stepped out of a boat and walked on water, and as long as he looked at Jesus, he was safe. Yet, "When he saw the wind boisterous, he began to sink" (see Matthew 14:28–30). Later, Peter looked at the Savior and said: "Thou art the Son of God," but when challenged by a maid he denied all knowledge of his Leader. Had he continued to think about his family, occupation, boat, nets and future, he might have remained in Capernaum. Simon was abandoning a good living to follow a homeless Carpenter and was leaving a comfortable home to be associated with One Who had no place to lay His head. Never again would he have a regular income; his future would be uncertain. Nevertheless, when Peter continued to look at Jesus, all his need was supplied.

Listening . . . *How Constructive*

"He taught them many things" (Mark 4:2).

The disciples had much to learn. The life which they were commencing would be different from anything they had known. According to Matthew, the men were among the first to hear the Sermon on the Mount, and to say the least, the principles enunciated therein were astonishing. Simon's reaction to the suggestions of the Lord can only be surmised. The nine benedictions mentioned by Jesus surely amazed Peter and the others in the congregation on the hillside. It was difficult to believe that the meek would inherit the earth, and if only the pure in heart would see God, there was little hope for anyone. Simon must have wondered about these doctrines. If an enemy compelled him to go one mile, he was expected to respond cheerfully by going twice the distance. If an obnoxious person struck him in the face, he was urged to turn the other cheek. This advice seemed to be preposterous, unreasonable, and inhuman. Yet these were the principles taught by the Master. Peter would do his best to obey, but would need a lot of assistance.

Learning . . . *How Convincing*

"Take my yoke upon you and learn of me: for I am meek and lowly in heart; and ye shall find rest unto your souls" (Matthew 11:29).

When the Lord called Matthew and dined with many of his friends, Simon Peter surely frowned. The tax collector was one of the most detested of Israel's citizens. He worked for the Romans and squeezed taxes from reluctant people. How could a decent God-fearing Hebrew fraternize with such a despicable fellow? Yet, it had become evident that Jesus desired his company and who could argue with the Lord? Simon Peter was aghast and frightened when a leper shouting "Unclean, Unclean," came running down the street to kneel at Jesus' feet. The man was an outcast from society and a menace to healthy people. He should have remained where he belonged! "And Jesus touched him." Horrors! That was too much. Speak to him from a safe distance, but touch him—never! If the disease spread they would all become inhabitants of the leper colony. The Lord probably smiled; Simon was learning fast. He had come not to destroy men's lives, but to heal and reclaim them.

Loving . . . *How Charming*

"He saith to him again . . . Simon, son of Jonas, Lovest thou me? He saith unto him, Yea, Lord, thou knowest that I love thee" (John 21:16).

It was impossible for a dedicated believer to remain with the Lord without experiencing the transforming power of His affection. The disciple-students were very imperfect, but the Teacher's patience and ability were inexhaustible. As the time passed, their improvement was phenomenal. The rugged, forthright fisherman from Galilee ultimately wrote to his friends, saying:

"And beside this, giving all diligence, add to your faith virtue; and to virtue knowledge; and to knowledge temperance; and to temperance patience, and to patience godliness; And to godliness brotherly kindness; and to brotherly kindness, charity" (2 Peter 1:5–7).

It is difficult to believe that the man who could be temperamental and unreliable could become the rock; that the coward frightened by a maid could be the inspired preacher at Pentecost; and the fisherman who abandoned his boat to follow an itinerant Preacher could say to a cripple at the gate of the temple: "Silver and gold have I none, but such as I have give I thee. In the name of Jesus Christ of Nazareth rise up and walk" (see Acts 3:6). Jesus was wise when He called these insignificant men. He might have called the most articulate scholars from the schools of learning, but He chose ordinary people who, in His sight, were unpolished diamonds. He valued them just as they were, but when their training had been completed, He had polished His jewels until each and every facet reflected the glory of God. The Lord was elated; His students were ready for ordination.

6

PETER'S ORDINATION TO PREACH THE GOSPEL

"And he ordained twelve that they should be with him, and that he might send them forth to preach, and to have power to heal sicknesses, and to cast out devils" (Mark 3:14–15).

The Savior resembled an evangelist selecting a committee to handle the details of a great crusade. Within this modern world of computers, fax, and other machines, many inconspicuous workers labor day and night to prepare for others who receive most of the fame. Without their invaluable assistance, the success of the venture might be in jeopardy. The Lord knew His untried disciples would be severely tested, and would be alone as they tried to solve their problems. Eventually, He would return whence He had come, and although the Holy Spirit would be an effective substitute, the apostles would need to become accustomed to the new leadership. Many years later John continued to remember the time when Jesus had accompanied them through the countryside. He wrote:

"That which was from the beginning, which we have heard, which we have seen with our eyes, which we have looked upon, and our hands have handled, of the Word of life; For the life was manifested, and we have seen it, and bear witness, and shew unto you that eternal life, which was with the Father, and was manifested unto us. That which we have seen and heard declare we unto you" (1 John 1:1–3).

The apostle John was like his friend, Simon Peter. He was thrilled the Holy Spirit had taken the place of the Savior, but continued to treasure memories of the days when he had leaned upon the Master's bosom (see John 13:23). The Lord realized He could not do everything alone, that dependable workers needed training before they could become involved in world evangelism. It was significant that Matthew, Mark and Luke agreed that of the twelve men, Simon Peter was the first to be selected.

The Amazing Privilege . . . *Chosen "to be with him"*

The Greek word translated *ordained* is *epoieesen*; it means appointed—set apart. The Lord set aside twelve men to be with Him. Probably the full and complete ordination came later when, after His resurrection, the Savior breathed on them, and said: "Receive ye the Holy Ghost" (see John 20:22). It might be claimed that coming events were casting their shadows before. Jesus knew the identity of the men who would become His ambassadors, and selected them early so that they could be specially trained for their task. The phrase "to be with him" is exceptionally thought-provoking. It suggests that what the disciples were *to* the Lord, was more important than anything they did *for* Him. Service is valuable in the extension of Christ's kingdom, but communion and fellowship are better. Working for the Savior can be stereotyped, formal, automatic and irksome. Communion is warm, wonderful and inspiring.

Christians who fail to commune with their Lord may work ceaselessly and yet accomplish little. The Lord needed and valued real friends. It was significant that the disciple who was truly appreciated by Jesus was he who leaned upon the Master's bosom. Unless believers make time to be *with Christ,* their quality of service will deteriorate. It was surprising that whereas twelve men were appointed to be *with Christ,* only three appeared to enjoy that privilege. Peter, James and John accompanied Him into the Mount of Transfiguration, the home of Jairus, and the Garden of Gethsemane (see Matthew 17:1; Luke 8:51; Matthew 26:37). The other disciples were conspicuous by their absence.

It is to be regretted that when these standards are applied to the church, the results are startling. Many professing Christians are too busy to climb a mountain with Christ; they prefer to remain in the valley watching television. Unfortunately, many never read the Scriptures; they prefer to read newspapers. The Savior desires fellowship with His people, and continues to call men and women to *be with Him.* When last did we see His face and feel the warmth of His embrace?

The Anointed Preaching . . . *Challenging "to preach"*

Preaching is the art and ability to tell people about Christ. The audience may be large or small, but to talk about the Savior is a responsibility delegated to Christians. All who claim allegiance to the Redeemer should share the privilege of informing others about Him. Preaching is the long arm of the church; it reaches all nations. It became evident to the disciples that their Master loved to speak about His Father and the necessity of being prepared to meet Him. The Bible tells how Christ preached in the villages and along the shores of the Sea of Galilee, where large crowds listened to His message and watched the miracles which He performed. When the need for more witnesses increased, the Lord called twelve disciples, and later invited seventy additional men to share the work of evangelism. If we add the seventy to the original twelve, and assume they were dispatched in pairs, there were forty-one teams of evangelists working simultaneously in the country. This was a very intense crusade operating in a small area. God was truly visiting His people but unfortunately "he came unto his own, and his own received him not" (see John 1:11).

It is interesting that none of the original twelve had received any theological training. They had neither a change of clothing nor spare money. They were told to inquire for worthy people, and to abide in their homes. They had no sponsors to defray expenses, and at one point in his life Simon Peter said to a cripple at the gate of the temple: "Silver and gold have I none, but such as I have, give I thee. In the name of Jesus Christ of Nazareth rise up and walk" (Acts 3:6). It was in this extraordinary fashion the Gospel was first proclaimed. It is worthy of attention that when the preachers returned from their assignment, they said: "Even the devils were subject unto us through thy Name" (Luke 10:17). It is difficult to believe that four fishermen from Galilee could lead an attack against the forces of evil. As far as is known not one of the disciples had even instructed a class in the synagogue; they were not gifted orators nor skilled educators. Their hands had been toughened by pulling nets, and they were experienced only in speaking to individual customers, or people who retailed their fish. Later, Paul was correct when he wrote:

"For ye see your calling, brethren, how that not many wise men after the flesh, not many mighty, not many noble are called. But God hath chosen the foolish things of the world to confound the wise; and God hath chosen the weak things of the world to confound the things which are mighty. And not base things of the world, and things which are despised hath God chosen, yea and things which are not, to bring to nought things which are. That no flesh should glory in his presence" (1 Corinthians 1:26–29).

The Awsome Power . . . *Curing "to heal all manner of diseases and to cast out devils"*

When Jesus sent forth His disciples, He said: "Behold I send you forth as sheep in the midst of wolves" (Matthew 10:16). Sheep and lambs are helpless when attacked by ferocious beasts. It was to be expected that the disciples would be unable to fulfill their assignment unless special ability was supplied by the Lord. They were to overcome the resistance of a pagan world, and destroy the influence of people who knew nothing about the saving grace of God. Without any military might they were to conquer armies. To do this would be impossible unless they were strengthened by the Lord. If the disciples had only preached to people, some may have argued, others remained indifferent, but most would have ignored what was said. Yet, when cripples began jumping for joy and blind men shouted "I can see, I can see," people began to pay attention. Some theologians argue that the promise of being able to heal the sick was not included in some of the older manuscripts. That would be of little, if any, consequence for other parts of the New Testament indicate those early preachers were able to heal suffering people. It was believed that all mental illness was the result of demon possession, and therefore when the disciples dealt with that problem, they gained the attention of everybody. The servants of Christ were excellent preachers of the Gospel; they did so by what they said; what they were; and what they did. All ministers should emulate their glorious example.

It appeared to be ridiculous to expect Andrew and Bartholomew, and lesser known disciples, to confront raging lunatics and restore sanity to people controlled by demons. Yet, the promise of the Savior guaranteed the success of their mission. No obstacle was too great to be overcome in the Name of Jesus. Nevertheless, without the enabling power of Christ, even the most talented man would be unable to prevail against the opposition which was sure to come. It may be argued that the work of the Christian church has more than fulfilled the promise made by the Savior. Doctors and nurses have taken their healing ministry to nations which for generations were deprived of medical assistance. Churches have been followed by hospitals and it cannot be denied most of the blessings of western civilization have been conveyed to suffering humanity through the ministry of the Christian church. Nevertheless, it is a cause for depression when the modern world seems more competent at building and maintaining mental institutions, than in expelling demons from afflicted people.

It is thrilling to know that ultimately there will be nothing to hurt in all God's holy mountain. Sin, sickness, and Satan will be eternally banished, and the earth shall be filled with the glory of the Lord, as the waters cover the sea. Simon Peter was one of those early preachers, but it can only be imagined how he felt when first he became aware of his ability to heal the sick, give sight to the blind, and deliverance to people enslaved by evil. He was becoming an expert at catching men for Christ.

7

THE SPOKESMAN FOR HIS COLLEAGUES

"And Jesus answered and said unto him, Blessed art thou, Simon Bar-jona . . ." (Matthew 16:17).

History suggests that some men are born to be leaders; others who are equally sincere are content to follow. Simon Peter was an excitable fellow who was active, impetuous and outspoken. Others chosen by the Savior were subdued and reserved. It was significant that at Pentecost eleven disciples stood with Peter. If their comrade succeeded, they would rejoice in his triumph; if he were killed, they would die with him. Not much was ever said about James, the son of Alphaeus, Simon Zelotes, or Judas the brother of James, but it is evident that in their own special way they played a vital part in establishing the kingdom of Christ. They were not envious of the attention given to Peter, for they were content to work quietly in the background. Simon was explosive and occasionally too hasty in word and deed. When others were content to reason carefully, he uttered the first words which came into his mind. This characteristic was seen throughout his career.

Peter Replying

"From that time many of his disciples went back, and walked no more with him. Then said Jesus unto the twelve, Will ye also go away? Then Simon Peter answered him, Lord, to whom shall we go? thou hast the words of eternal life" (John 6:67–68).

When some of the people refused to believe what the Lord had said, He replied: "What, and if ye shall see the Son of man ascending up where he was?" The inference became obvious. Jesus was expressing His pre-existence. He had been in eternity with God, and had descended to earth to perform a special mission. Eventually He would return whence He had come. Some of the listeners scowled;

their eyes reflected unbelief. Even Christ's miracles began to fade into insignificance, and shaking their heads, the critics began to depart. It was depressing to see the people leaving. Jesus sighed and said to those remaining, "Will ye also go away?" While the other disciples remained silent, Simon Peter answered: "To whom can we go? Thou hast the words of eternal life." His statement was informative, for it signified he believed the message of salvation to be more important than anything else in the world.

Simon Peter seemed to be saying: "Master, if we searched everywhere we would never find a greater teacher. If You were missing, the world would be empty." Probably the other disciples were convinced of the same fact, but only Peter confessed his convictions. He would have loved a modern hymn:

> All that I need is in Jesus.
> He satisfies; joy He supplies.
> Life would be worthless without Him.
> All things in Jesus I find.

Peter Reminding

"Then Peter began to say unto him, Lo, we have left all and have followed thee" (Mark 10:28).

The disciples were dumbfounded! They had watched a young man rejecting their Master. He had chosen between discipleship and wealth. Unfortunately, the ruler decided his money was more desirable. When the Lord quietly said, "It is easier for a camel to go through the eye of a needle than for a rich man to enter into the kingdom of God" the disciples exclaimed, "Who then can be saved?" The eye of a needle was the name given to the small door in the gate of the city. When the large entrance was closed at sunset, the door remained open for pedestrians. Occasionally, travelers tried to squeeze animals through the opening, but the task was impossible unless the camel was made to kneel, and its burdens removed. Unfortunately, the rich young ruler did not bow in submission to the Savior, and was unwilling to abandon his wealth. Peter frowned and said: "But, Lord, we were wiser. We were not wealthy, but such as we possessed we abandoned to become your disciples. Furthermore, we would do it again if that became necessary."

"And Jesus answered and said, Verily I say unto you, There is no man that hath left house, or brethren, or sisters, or father, or mother, or wife or children, or lands, for my sake, and the gospel's, but he shall receive an hundredfold now in this time houses, and brethren, and sisters, and mothers, and children, and lands, with persecutions; and in the world to come eternal life" (Mark 10:29–30).

The Savior emphasized that God always gives more than He receives. He is no man's debtor. This information might not have been supplied had not Peter expressed what his colleagues were only thinking.

Peter Reasoning

"And when they were come to Capernaum, they that received tribute money came to Peter, and said, Doth not your master pay tribute? He said, Yes. And when he was come into the house, Jesus prevented him, saying, What thinkest thou Simon? of whom do the kings of the earth take custom or tribute? of their own children, or of strangers?" (Matthew 17:24–25).

Simon Peter was worried; a tribute collector had asked if Jesus paid His dues to the temple authorities; and without prior thought, he had answered affirmatively. Now he was troubled because he might have been untruthful. There has been confusion concerning this story; the tax had not been levied by King Herod or Caesar; it was a means of raising money for the upkeep and support of the temple. The *didachma* was a silver coin which equaled, in Jewish money, one half shekel of silver. Today, it might be worth a half dollar. The money was stored in the temple treasury, and was used partly for the purchase of sacrifices, incense, and the remuneration of rabbis and other officials. There was always a large surplus which became a temptation to greedy conquerors. It is recorded that Cressus (54 B.C.) stole the equivalent of more than ten million dollars. Every male over twenty years of age was expected to pay and during the ministry of Jesus, early in each year, special collecting booths were erected in every community.

The commandment was first given by Moses, when the money was used for the erection and decoration of the Tabernacle. The amount stipulated was a half shekel of silver (see Exodus 30:11–13).

After the Hebrews returned from Babylon, it was changed to one-third of a shekel. This might have been necessary because of the impoverishment of the former captives (see Nehemiah 10:32). That was the tax or tribute to which the collector referred. After Peter had replied to the man's question, he was not sure his answer had been correct. Jesus knew His friend was troubled, and asked: "What thinkest thou, Simon?" Then before an answer could be forthcoming, He continued: "Of whom do the kings of the earth take custom or tribute, of their own children or of strangers? Would an earthly monarch expect his family to pay taxes to support the royal household?" Peter probably answered, "From strangers, Lord." "Then why should the Son of God be expected to pay for the upkeep of His Father's house?" Peter was being taught an important lesson, but as he listened Jesus said: "Notwithstanding, lest we should offend them, go thou to the sea, and cast an hook, and take up the fish that first cometh up, and when thou hast opened his mouth, thou shalt find a piece of money; that take and give unto them for me and for thee" (Matthew 17:27).

Peter did as he was commanded, but what he expected to find on his fishing expedition can only be imagined. He baited a hook and cast it into the water. Feeling a tug on the line, he pulled in the fish and gasped when he saw the silver coin in its mouth. Formerly, cynics laughed at this account, but they no longer dismiss it as fantasy. The finding of coins in the mouths of fish is no longer considered to be miraculous. Through the medium of television, people have seen great numbers of tiny fish darting into their mother's mouth when a predator approaches. They emerge only when the enemy has departed. Peter's miracle was twofold. Jesus stated the coin would be in the mouth of the FIRST fish to be caught; he would not have to wait for the right fish to arrive. Furthermore, the Lord knew the value of the coin, for He said: "That take and give unto them for me and for thee." Evidently Simon had not paid his tax; the Lord paid it for him! Probably the Big Fisherman often referred to that strange event, and throughout his ministry proudly explained that on two special occasions his debt had been paid by the Savior.

Peter Requesting

"Then answered Peter, and said unto Jesus, Lord, it is good for us to be here. If thou wilt, let us make three tabernacles; one for thee, and one for Moses, and one for Elias" (Matthew 17:4).

It is difficult to decide whether Peter's request deserved condemnation or praise. Was he trying to protect the Lord, or being kind to himself? Down in the valley the crowds were becoming hostile; the Pharisees were critical, and it seemed the Master was wasting His time. He was predicting His death, and the outlook was becoming increasingly bleak. When Peter recognized Moses and Elijah, the mountain seemingly became a holy place. He said: "Lord, let us stay here indefinitely. The people in the city are unworthy of your benediction; they are critical, unappreciative, and cannot be trusted. There is great danger in the valley. Let us remain here until the situation changes."

That request had merit, and yet, on the other hand, it might have been thoughtless, hasty, and selfish; Peter might have been thinking only of himself. He was enjoying his first glimpse of Heaven; why should his ecstasy terminate so quickly? Perhaps had he not been so self-centered he might have recognized there was no apparent need on the hillside, whereas many people who needed a healing touch were waiting in the valley. If the small party remained where they were, lepers would die, blind beggars would remain in darkness, and redemption for mankind would never be provided. Peter's enthusiasm had run away with his brain! Once again he was being impulsive, and it was providential that God interrupted his request by telling him to pay attention to Jesus (Matthew 17:4–5). It is always better to listen carefully than to speak unwisely. When the illustrious visitors departed, the disciples "saw no man, save Jesus only" (Matthew 17:8). That was one of the most inspiring moments during the ministry of the Lord. The law and the prophets were wonderful, but the Son of God was infinitely greater. When all else ceased to be, He remained; no other could take His place. Poor Peter—when he opened his mouth, he often put his foot into it!

Peter Responding

"Then came Peter to him and said, Lord, how oft shall my brother sin against me, and I forgive him? till seven times? Jesus saith unto him, I say not unto thee until seven times; but until seventy times seven" (Matthew 18:21–22).

Simon Peter was nonplussed! His brain was reeling; he needed a large computer! The Lord had proposed a course of action which was apparently beyond the bounds of possibility. The disciple had asked how many times he would be expected to forgive an offending brother, and with tongue in cheek, had suggested seven times. To be fair to the Big Fisherman, let it be admitted the number mentioned was not easily attained. To forgive a man for striking one in the face would indicate grace; but to do so repeatedly, perhaps would indicate folly. Jesus had suggested that if someone had a grievance, a deputation of church members should interview him in the hope of settling the matter peacefully. If this effort failed, the offending man should be excommunicated. All this was intriguing to Simon Peter, but he would have preferred to remove the man by physical force. He might have exclaimed: "Throw him out and forget him." Possibly the Master would have prevented this. Peter reasoned: "There must be a limit to everything; some of these people believe they are without fault. How long am I expected to tolerate offensive behavior? Would seven times be sufficient?"

The Savior said: "Peter, sit down and let me tell you a story. There was a certain man who held a very important office within a kingdom. He was the Minister of Finance who stole ten thousand talents. [If the talents were in gold, the modern equivalent would be in excess of $260 million.] He was charged with embezzlement and sentenced by his king. Yet, when the guilty man begged for pardon, it was granted. The same official had a servant who owed him one hundred pence [less than five dollars]. When the servant begged for forgiveness and promised to repay the money, the man refused to be compassionate and threw the offender into prison. When the king heard of this he became very angry and rescinded what had been previously arranged."

The hundred pence owed by the servant was less than five dollars, and it seems incredible that he who had been forgiven so much should be reluctant to cancel such a small debt. Even the language used by the Lord indicates the vicious character of this unforgiving man, for *he took his victim by the throat* as if to strangle him. We must remember that Peter had spoken of the possibility of forgiving seven times, and had been told by Jesus that seventy times seven would be a more appropriate figure. If we super-impose these facts upon the illustration given by Jesus, we discover the enormity of the offense of the unforgiving dignitary. Having been forgiven a sum of money in excess of millions of dollars, he refused to forgive a debt which was very insignificant. Had he been more gracious, he would have recognized his need to forgive—not seventy times seven, but at

46

the very least, *three hundred thousand times seven*. It might have been even more, for it is difficult to know fully how great had been his own debt.

These staggering figures were really not of overwhelming importance. It was the thought behind the story which became paramount. Jesus was reminding His disciples that God had already forgiven them many millions of dollars worth of sins! His unfailing mercy had canceled their debt. If they had been forgiven so much, they should be more than willing to forgive any brother or sister whose debt was minimal. Peter needed a computer to unravel all the suggested financial problems, but the prevailing fact was obvious. It would be easier to continue forgiving everybody. A lifetime of perpetual pardoning would be too short for Peter to forgive others what God had already forgiven him (see the author's commentary, *Matthew's Majestic Gospel*, Kregel Publications, Grand Rapids, Michigan).

This remarkable story indicates the immensity of God's pardoning grace, and brings to mind the question asked by Micah: "Who is a God like unto thee, that pardoneth iniquity, and passeth by the transgression of the remnant of his heritage? he retaineth not his anger forever, because he delighteth in mercy" (see Micah 7:18). "Peter, you owed God an immense debt. Never be hard on your brethren if they hurt you. You never catch fish by throwing bricks at them."

"And be ye kind one to another, tenderhearted, forgiving one another even as God for Christ's sake hath forgiven you" (Ephesians 4:32).

8

HOW SIMON PETER
STARTED A BALL ROLLING

"And Simon Peter answered and said, Thou art the Christ, the Son of the Living God" (Matthew 16:16).

The impact made by Jesus of Nazareth upon the villages of Palestine was remarkable. When He arrived in a community, business came to an abrupt halt as all the people hastened to hear the Man Who had become the subject of every conversation. The Lord knew what was taking place, and one day, said to His disciples: "Whom do men say that I am?" That question might have seemed unnecessary, for it was said "He knew what was in man" (see John 2:25). The Lord, Who was able to read the thoughts of men and women, had an ulterior motive when He asked His question. The disciples said, "Master, some of the people believe you to be John the Baptist and Elijah; others mention Jeremiah, but all agree you are a prophet. John and Elijah were great preachers, and Jeremiah was saddened by the sinfulness of the nation. Some of these men have come to the conclusion that You must be one of the prophets." Maybe the Lord's eyes were sparkling when He said: "But whom do ye say that I am?"

> "And Simon Peter answered and said, Thou art the Christ, the Son of the living God. And Jesus answered and said unto him, Blessed art thou, Simon Bar-jona, for flesh and blood hath not revealed it unto thee, but my Father which is in heaven" (Matthew 16:16–17).

If angels heard this glorious statement made by Simon Peter, they might have filled heaven with applause. He had been an attentive student in God's academy, and had learned facts which enriched him forever. During the years to come many other people would express opinions concerning the Savior, but no statement would supersede the one made by the fisherman from Galilee. The beloved John and others would have much to say about the deity of Christ, and the fourth Gospel would emphasize the Word was in the beginning with God, and truly was God. Nevertheless, not even John learned that fact more quickly than Simon Peter. His revelation came as a flash of lightning in the darkness of a human mind. Nothing else could have produced such assurance.

The Lord said: "Blessed art thou, Simon Bar-jona. Happy, privileged, favored art thou, Simon. My Father must be glad that He was able to impart such knowledge. Now let me tell you something else."

> " . . . thou art Peter, [Petros], and upon this rock [petra] I will build my church; and the gates of hell shall not prevail against it" (Matthew 16:18).

That startling announcement was destined to become the most discussed statement ever made by the Savior. It gave birth to the Roman Catholic Church, in which millions of devout people sincerely believe the church of Jesus Christ is built upon the rock—Simon Peter. However, during recent years a remarkable change has taken place in the thinking of Catholic theologians; they now deny what they formerly believed. One of their leaders who appeared on Canadian television was asked to explain the charismatic upheaval which had revolutionized the thinking of his colleagues. He said: "We have come to understand that certain Scripture verses do not mean what we thought they did." It is now admitted that even at his best, Simon Peter would be a very shaky foundation for the universal church of the living Christ.

It is informative to note two Greek words used by the Lord. He said: "Thou art Peter [Petros]—a stone. The word is masculine. "Upon this rock [Petra] I will build my church . . . ." This word is feminine. The Rock is the source from which the stone is produced. Christ is the rock of ages; He produces the stone. "Peter, you will become part of, and even a leader in the Assembly which will rest upon this solid foundation. Within the church you and others will exercise great authority; what you do on earth will be ratified in Heaven." It is to be regretted that every artist's picture of Simon Peter depicts him having a key—which supposedly unlocks Heaven's gate. Upon this false interpretation rests the theology of the Catholic Church. Until recently it was taught that unless the apostle Peter unlocked Heaven's door, entry was impossible. I shall never forget an open-air Gospel meeting held in the city of Glasgow. A young man was preaching about the text: "I am the door" when an obstinate heckler yelled: "Yes, Jesus is the door, but Peter holds the key." With a flash of brilliance the preacher replied: "Thank God, we do not need a key—the door is open."

1. Peter was never meant to be the foundation upon which the church would be erected. "For other foundation can no man lay than that is laid, which is Jesus Christ" (1 Corinthians 3:11).

2. Peter was not even the leader of the apostles. The apostle who presided over the first church council was James. "And after they had held their peace, James answered, saying, Men and brethren, hearken unto me" (Acts 15:13).

3. Peter was not the one who opened the kingdom to the Gentile world. That privilege was given to Paul. "And [the Lord] said unto me, Depart: for I will send thee far hence unto the Gentiles" (Acts 22:21). "But the Lord said unto [Ananias], Go thy way; for [Saul] is a chosen vessel unto me, to bear my name before the Gentiles" (Acts 9:15).

4. Peter was not the only apostle to whom the gift of remitting sins was granted. "And when [Jesus] had said this, he breathed on them, and saith unto them, Receive ye the Holy Ghost: Whosoever sins ye remit, they are remitted unto them; and whosoever sins ye retain, they are retained" (John 20:22–23).

It must be recognized that the teaching which claims Peter was the source of apostolic succession, the basis upon which Roman Catholic doctrines rest, is erroneous. To assert that priests, descending from Peter alone, have the right of absolving sin is false, misleading and wrong. Andrew, Bartholomew, or any other of the apostles could have given birth to his own version of apostolic succession.

Arno C. Gaebelein has an interesting paragraph in his exposition of Matthew's Gospel. He writes, "What then does the Lord mean when He says, 'Thou art Peter and upon *this rock* will I build My assembly [church]?' He did not mean Peter or He would have said, 'upon THEE will I build My church.' The word Peter—*petros*, means a part of a rock; that is, a stone. When the Lord says upon what He is going to build His church, He no longer speaks of *petros*—a stone, but uses the word *petra*, which means 'a rock.' Out of the rock a stone is hewn; in other words, *a stone is a part of the rock*. The word *petra*—a rock, He uses for the first time in Matthew 7:24–25. The house there is built upon a *petra*—a rock, and cannot fall. This rock is Christ Himself. But why this peculiar use of *petros* and *petra*—a part of a rock, and the rock itself? Let Peter answer, 'To whom [Christ] coming, as unto *a living stone*, disallowed indeed of men, but chosen of God, and precious, Ye also *as lively stones*, are built up a spiritual house' (1 Peter 2:4–6). The foundation of God's building is Christ. Peter's confession said, 'Thou art the Christ, the Son of the living God.'" "Other foundation can no man lay." Peter, a stone hewn from a parent rock, is like any other believer; one of the stones in the spiritual edifice, resting upon the solid rock, the Lord Jesus Christ.

"Upon this rock I will build my church; and the gates of hell shall not prevail against it" (v. 18b). The term "my church" refers to that spiritual building which belongs exclusively to the Savior, and any other interpretation is unpardonable. The narrow, confined limits of religious legalism are something to be deplored. Catholic priests still teach that unless a man belongs to their church he is not within the true fold of God. The leaders of Protestant sects have become equally guilty, for they insist, as they criticize all other bodies of Christians, that their assembly alone is pleasing to God. There are churches where no baptism is recognized except that administered by their own clergymen; any ordinance celebrated elsewhere is classed as alien baptism. They resemble the Scribes and Pharisees, who created innumerable regulations not related to the will of the Lord. Thank God, when we reach Heaven it will be impossible to find a denominational church. We shall be too wise to argue about details of law. God's true church is an institution erected on the finished work of Christ, and all who love the Savior enjoy its fellowship (see the author's commentary, *Matthew's Majestic Gospel*, Kregel Publications, Grand Rapids, Michigan).

The Church of the Lord Jesus Christ is the greatest institution in existence. It contains people of all nationalities and color. Wealth cannot purchase membership, neither can poverty exclude the impoverished. The one basic qualification for membership is to be redeemed and cleansed by the precious blood of Christ; all who yield themselves to the Son of God are assured of acceptance. This church which was planned by the Divine Family cannot fail in its mission, for even the gates of hell cannot prevail against it. The time is approaching when witchcraft will disappear from the world; crime will be unknown in the streets of America; hospitals will close forever; and the love of God will unite the nations of the world. Individual denominations may flourish for a time then fall into obscurity, but the true church will continue eternally. It will be known as the Bride of Christ; the illustrious company of people for whom the Savior died. Happy is the person who belongs to that glorious assembly.

9

SIMON PETER'S DISLIKE
OF WHAT HE HEARD

"From that time forth began Jesus to shew unto his disciples, how that he must go unto Jerusalem and suffer many things of the elders and chief priests and scribes, and be killed, and be raised again the third day. Then Peter took him, and began to rebuke him, saying, Be it far from thee, Lord. This shall not be unto thee" (Matthew 16:21–22).

The Savior had reached a turning point in His ministry. The disciples had been partially trained for their ministry, but the moment had arrived when the men were to be made aware of unpleasant events which lay ahead. They had been thrilled as they contemplated the glory of the coming kingdom, and had commenced planning what they would do when their beloved Master sat upon the throne of David. Somehow those illusions had to be dispelled, and the Cross with all its ignominy and shame had to be introduced to their thinking. They had been expecting a crown of gold; it was essential to begin considering one of thorns. Instead of teaching by parables, Jesus began to speak clearly of His inevitable sufferings. As surprise spread across the faces of the listeners, Simon Peter became disturbed. Translating the text used by Matthew, *The Amplified Version of the Bible* says: "Then Peter took Him aside to speak with Him privately, and began to reprove Him, and charge Him sharply, saying, God forbid it. This must not happen to you. But Jesus turned away from Peter, and said unto him, Get behind me, Satan. You are in my way, an offense and a hindrance, and a snare to Me, for you are minding what partakes not of the nature and quality of God, but of men." Once again Peter had opened his mouth and put his foot into it!

Yet, it is not easy to criticize him. When people express fear of the future, it is customary for clergymen and other friends to urge people to trust in God; to permit faith to expel fear. The Greek word used was *epitiman* which suggests harsh criticism. Peter did not like what he had heard, and unwittingly became Satan's advocate. Turning away from His friend, the Lord addressed a reply, not to Simon Peter, but to the Devil who had used the disciple to express something contrary to the will of God.

How Careful Christians Should Be

This incident in the life of Peter should be considered carefully. The disciple's sincerity cannot be questioned, but the fact remains that for a short period of time, he permitted Satan to control his tongue, to suggest something contrary to the will of God. If the Lord had agreed with Peter, the plan of salvation would have been thwarted. Reconciliation through the crucifixion was the center of the divine purpose and the one thing which Satan feared. When the Lord was tempted, the devil offered to withdraw all opposition and make the conquest of the nations easy, if the Lord would bow in submission. Jesus rejected that proposal, believing as is now said: "The longest way around, sometimes is the shortest way home." Christ was the Lamb slain before the foundation of the world (see Revelation 13:8). "Who for the joy that was set before him endured the cross, despising the shame, and is set down at the right hand of the throne of God" (see Hebrews 12:2). The tongue of the Christian should be controlled by Christ; otherwise it may become an unruly member of the body (compare James 3:8).

How Consecrated Christians Need to Be

"Then said Jesus unto his disciples, If any man will come after me, let him deny himself and take up his cross, and follow me" (Matthew 16:24).

A modern song suggests it is good to dream, for otherwise a dreamer will never have one come true. There are occasions when fantasies enable people to surmount difficulties, forget problems, and for a few moments at least, live in wonderland. Probably this had already been true in the experience of the followers of Jesus. They had seen unprecedented miracles, and hardly knew what to expect next. Jesus was the Blessed One, the King of Israel, the Savior of the world. They seemed to be walking on air when, with devastating directness, the Lord shattered their dreams. He spoke of self-denial, the need of carrying a cross, and this appeared to be the harbinger of doom.

It was natural for people to desire the best in life and embrace every opportunity which promised prosperity. The idea of self-denial to promote something detested was contrary to reason. It seemed preposterous that Jesus should abandon the idea of establishing a kingdom, and even more ludicrous that the disciples should encourage Him to do so. Yet, their Master was deadly serious, emphasizing every word uttered. Their fantasies had been dispelled. The summer of delight had ended, and the winds of approaching winter made them shiver with apprehension. Peter, who had already been rebuked, was whispering to himself: "God forbid, this must not be."

Thus did the great Teacher introduce His students to the more difficult part of their training, and prepare them for service in an unappreciative world. Difficult days would come when adversity would test their loyalty, but above the clouds the sun continued to shine and would eventually reappear. If they stayed close to their Leader, the outlook could never be too bleak, for "whosoever followed Him would not walk in darkness but should have the light of life." Unconsecrated people could not succeed in their mission, and therefore the Lord was making sure His friends understood what it meant to be a true disciple.

How Convinced Christians Ought to Be

"For whosoever will save his life shall lose it; and whosoever will lose his life for my sake shall find it" (Matthew 16:25).

Life is probably the most valued treasure in the world. Unless illness, pain or shame diminishes the desire to live, no one desires death. The Master knew that some of His followers would become martyrs, and others who had followed Him for a time, would renounce their faith to avoid execution. Therefore, He made a distinction between mortal and eternal life, and explained the necessity of choosing wisely. People may live to be of great age, but on the other hand might die young. Eternal life is endless. Christ affirmed that to lose one's life for His sake would merely be an exchange of one thing for something more wonderful. Mortal existence would be replaced by something imperishable. Probably Jesus emphasized the words "for my sake"; to die for any other reason would not guarantee an entrance into the kingdom of God. Christians who died for their faith exhibited a great love for the Redeemer; they believed there was something more desirable than residing upon earth. Some treasures may seem irreplaceable. The late Dr. Frank Boreham said: "If you have anything without which you cannot live, GIVE IT AWAY." Jesus said: "If any man will come after me, let him deny himself, and take up his cross, and follow me" (Matthew 16:24).

The Lord was endeavoring to teach that whatever they might have abandoned He remained; and possessing Christ, they would be enriched immeasurably. Simon Peter had already reminded the Lord of the sacrifice he and the others had made to become disciples. They had left home, families, friends, occupation and fishing boats to become disciples, but they had gained more than they had lost. True wealth was not in something accumulated, but in fellowship with the Son of God. When a man lost his soul in pursuing riches, he was not only a poor business man; he was foolish.

Within a short time James, the brother of John, would be murdered by King Herod (Acts 12:2); Stephen would be stoned by an angry mob, and later, Peter would be crucified. The saints who would die for their faith had the confidence they were losing little to obtain much, and this became evident in their testimony. Stephen, when he was dying, said: "Behold see the heaven opened, and the Son of man standing on the right hand of God" (see Acts 7:56). Paul, prior to his execution, wrote: "Henceforth there is laid up for me a crown of righteousness which the Lord, the righteous judge, shall give me at that day; and not to me only, but unto all them that love his appearing" (see 2 Timothy 4:8).

How Content Christians Must Be

"For the son of man shall come in the glory of his Father with his angels; and then he shall reward every man according to his works" (Matthew 16:27).

The brightest star in the Christian's sky is the promise of Christ's return. Circumstances may be discouraging, and opposition fierce, but this should never obscure the fact that the Savior will become the King of Kings and Lord of Lords. Paul was correct when he wrote: "For I reckon that the sufferings of this present time are not worthy to be compared with the glory that shall be revealed in us" (see Romans 8:18). People who trust in Christ should first look back, then up, within, around and onward, and should be able to see in every direction the grace of God. This should be evident in the ministry of every preacher. Simon Peter needed to learn these facts for upon his shoulders would rest the responsibility of being God's messenger at Pentecost. The Lord was sowing seed which would produce an astonishing harvest. Equipped by the Master, Simon Peter realized the immensity of his privilege. He knew that redemption had been made possible by the sacrifice of the Savior, but rewards would only be given to those who faithfully served Christ. When Jesus returns, "He will reward every man according to his work."

How Condemned Critics Will Be

"Verily I say unto you, there be some standing here which will not taste of death, till they see the Son of man coming in his kingdom" (Matthew 16:28).

HOMILY NO. 3

Christ . . . *and the nastiest taste in the world (Hebrews 2:9)*

The term *death* has a threefold interpretation in the Scriptures. (1) Death is the termination of life's earthly journey. It is the experience which, through sickness, accident, or age, eventually overcomes man and removes him from conscious association with fellow beings. (2) Death is used to express the state of unregenerate men. They are said to be dead in trespasses and sins, and by that term is inferred the fact that they are unresponsive to the prompting of the Spirit of God. (3) Death is the ultimate tragedy which overwhelms the guilty. When a sinful world appears before the throne of God, each man will be judged according to the facts written in God's records. "And they were judged every man according to their works. And death and hell were cast into the lake of fire. This is the second death" (Revelation 20:13–14). There are certain texts of Holy Scripture which can only be understood as they are examined in the light of these facts.

Death and the Critics

And the Lord Jesus said, "Verily I say unto you, There be some standing here, which shall not taste of death, till they see the Son of man coming in his kingdom" (Matthew 16:28). This was an outstanding utterance, and can mean only one thing. It will be immediately recognized that neither of the first two interpretations could

57

possibly explain the text. The people to whom Christ referred were hypocrites, and were said to be "whited sepulchres"; bigoted zealots who were expert at finding faults in all hearts but their own. They were already dead in sin. We do not know how long they survived, but it is perfectly safe to say they were buried long ago; while the promise of Christ's coming still awaits fulfillment. It follows that the only possible interpretation of the text is one which takes our thoughts into the future. Christ realized the undying hatred of His enemies, and boldly pronounced that before final doom overtook His critics, they would witness His triumph. And in that one statement He reaffirmed His belief in the survival of the soul. He recognized that physical death is not annihilation, but an introduction to a new world. He also declared His belief in the final judgment. "They shall not taste of death *till* they see the Son of man coming in his kingdom."

Death and the Christ

"But we see Jesus, who was made a little lower than the angels for the suffering of death, crowned with glory and honour; that he by the grace of God *should taste death for every man*" (Hebrews 2:9). The Lord Jesus was never dead in sins, for "he was in all points tempted like as we are, yet without sin" (4:15). And it is also extremely difficult to understand how His succumbing to physical weakness could materially affect every man. Unless there is spiritual truth connected with His sacrifice, then a death two thousand years ago could hardly affect modern people. The second death means separation from God; a state of inexpressible remorse; the outcome of lost opportunities; the inevitable reward of sin. "Christ tasted death for every man." He took our sins and went into the darkness. When the three hours of impenetrable blackness gave place to the new dawn, Christ uttered a cry of glad relief. He said, "My God, my God, why *didst* thou forsake me?" The aorist tense of the verb is used in this connection, revealing something completely accomplished in the past. The work was finished; the struggle had ended. Christ had been in the dark so that we could remain in the light forever.

Death and the Christian

"'Then said the Jews unto him, Now we know that thou hast a devil. Abraham is dead, and the prophets; and thou sayest, If a man keep my saying, *he shall never taste of death*' (John 8:52). It is not difficult to appreciate the problems of those Jewish hearers. It seemed fantastic that this Carpenter should speak such apparent absurdities. Yet, as Paul afterward declared: 'These things are spiritually discerned.' Jesus said unto Martha: 'I am the resurrection, and the life: he that believeth in me, though he were dead, yet shall he live: And whosoever liveth and believeth in me, shall never die' (John 11:25–26). Once again two interpretations are instantly ruled out. Since we were born in sin and shaped in iniquity, and since countless thousands of saints have passed through the valley of the shadow of death, the text can only mean one thing. The Christian will never know the anguish of eternal condemnation, because in Christ he has been pardoned. The Lord Jesus said, 'They shall not come into condemnation' (John 5:24). We shall never taste the bitterness of eternal death, because He tasted it for us." (Copied from the author's *Bible Treasures*, Kregel Publications, Grand Rapids, Michigan.)

10

MEMBERS OF CHRIST'S CABINET

"And after six days Jesus taketh Peter, James and John his brother, and bringeth them up into an high mountain apart" (Matthew 17:1).

Within the early church were many active workers and twelve apostles whom the Lord chose to become His cabinet. When and how Peter, James and John were elevated to that position was never revealed, but it seems evident that the Savior honored them with distinction. These men exhibited keener interest in the welfare of their Master, and accompanied Him on auspicious occasions. They were with Him on the Mount of Transfiguration, in the home of Jairus when the ruler's daughter was raised from the dead, and in the Garden of Gethsemane when the Master's perspiration fell as blood to the ground.

There are many unanswered questions regarding these events. Were Peter and the others specially selected by the Lord to be His intimate companions? It is interesting that no complaint was ever uttered by the other disciples; they were not jealous of the honors given to their brethren. Did the remaining nine men prefer the food and fellowship available in the homes of friends while their colleagues climbed the mountain with Christ? Did they desire a night of fellowship rather than one of intercession? The inner circle saw and heard many things which the others did not; the associations in the valley could never compensate for the ecstasy known by their comrades. Simon Peter became God's spokesman at Pentecost; John became the esteemed father of the churches, and James, the first to lay down his life for the Master (Acts 12:2). He surely received a great welcome when he reached his eternal home. Perhaps the experiences of those privileged men may be summarized under three headings.

The Hillside Of Splendor . . . *How Majestic*

"And it came to pass about eight days after these sayings, he took Peter and John and James, and went up into a mountain to pray. And as he prayed, the fashion of his countenance was altered, and his raiment was white and glistening" (Luke 9:28–29).

It is irrefutable that certain events in life are forgotten quickly; others remain in our memories forever. Many things happened during the ministry of the Savior, which seemed unforgettable, but with time were forgotten. One event stood out more clearly for Simon Peter than any other. More than thirty years after the transfiguration of the Lord, the apostle remembered clearly what happened on that memorable occasion. He wrote:

"For we have not followed cunningly devised fables, when we made known unto you the power and coming of our Lord Jesus Christ, but were eyewitnesses of his majesty. For he received from God the Father honour and glory when there came such a voice to him from the excellent glory: This is my beloved Son in whom I am well pleased. And this voice which came from heaven we heard, when we were with him in the holy mount" (2 Peter 1:16–18).

When the apostle wrote those words he was becoming an old man, but he remembered clearly the day when he saw the glory of Christ and the radiant messengers with whom He spoke in the holy mountain. It might be significant that Peter was the only one of the apostles who mentioned this occurrence in the books which they wrote.

The Unforgettable Christ

"And he prayed, the fashion of his countenance was altered and his raiment was white and glistening" (Luke 9:29).

It is not known when the three disciples fell asleep, but when they awakened they were astonished to see the transfigured Savior. Radiance was emanating from His soul, and even his garments were resplendent. Peter had never witnessed such a sight, and it was never repeated until after the resurrection. Evidently, Jesus belonged to another world.

The Undisclosed Conversation

Moses and Elijah appeared to be sharing the radiance of the Savior. As the disciples listened they realized the conversation was about something which would happen in Jerusalem. "They spake of his decease which he would accomplish at Jerusalem." The Lord had already predicted His crucifixion, but that was something which would happen to Him. He would be crucified and buried. The two visitors appeared to be emphasizing what Jesus would accomplish. His resurrection would be a triumph, but the patriarchs spoke about something to be accomplished *WHEN HE DIED.* "They spake of his decease." The crucifixion would not be a tragedy, the outcome of Jewish hatred, but a triumph applauded by angels. Paul wrote: "And having spoiled principalities and powers, he made a shew of them openly, triumphing over them in it" (Colossians 2:15). The resurrection was God saying "AMEN" to what had been accomplished at Calvary. The fact that Moses and Elijah spoke of the death of the Lord, suggests the inhabitants of God's eternal world were aware of events taking place on earth. They understood the purposes of the Almighty.

The Unmistakable Command

When God said: "This is my beloved Son in whom I am well pleased," the attention of heaven and earth was directed toward Jesus—the Divine Spokesman. That message still applies. Men often speak of a chain of command, but that idea may be seen in the Scripture. God spoke through His Son; Jesus spoke through His disciples, and they through their writings—THE BIBLE. Wise men shun arguments—they prefer to listen.

The House Of Sorrow . . . *How Miserable*

"And when he came into the house, he suffered no man to go in, save Peter, and James, and John, and the father and the mother of the maiden. And all wept, and bewailed her, but he said, Weep not, she is not dead, but sleepeth. And they laughed him to scorn, knowing that she was dead" (Luke 8:51–53).

It would be enlightening if it were known why Simon Peter and his friends were invited to accompany the Lord into the home of Jairus. People were excited because the ruler of the synagogue had sought assistance from the Nazarene. A daughter of twelve years lay seriously ill, and dreading death, the worried father had publicly knelt at the feet of the Man against whom he had warned his congregation. His request had been favorably received, and a great crowd was following the Savior when an unexpected interruption halted the procession. An afflicted woman who had spent all her money paying doctors' bills, had touched the hem of Christ's garment and had been instantly healed. When Simon and the other disciples heard the Lord asking: "Who touched me?" they were astonished, but once again it was Peter who expressed what the others thought.

"Master, that is a strange question. You have been pushing your way through this great crowd, and within the last fifty yards, dozens of people touched You." The Lord replied: "Somebody TOUCHED Me. I knew it the moment virtue went out of me." Peter was being specially trained to do a Herculean task, and needed to be reminded God cared for an impoverished woman who apparently had few if any friends. No one can explain a miracle; it has to be accepted by people who realize with God nothing is impossible.

When Jesus eventually arrived at the home of Jairus, He heard the chants of the minstrels and saw the professional mourners whose tears were meaningless. When the hubbub had ceased and the noisy performers expelled, Jesus said to His special friends: "Come with Me," and accompanied by the grieving parents, He proceeded to the bedside of the child. Within a few moments she was in the embrace of her parents. It may never be known how this incident fitted into the pattern of Peter's training. Nothing was beyond the capability of his Master. He had been taught a very important lesson. The best thing to do with a problem was to share it with Jesus. The woman who had touched Christ's garment and the distraught father knew that fact, but it took a little longer for Simon Peter to learn it.

The Holiness of the Savior ... *How Marvelous*

"And they came to a place which was named Gethsemane: and he saith to his disciples, Sit ye here, while I shall pray. And he taketh with him Peter, and James, and John and began to be sore amazed, and to be very heavy [downcast]" (Mark 14:32–33).

It is difficult to know how much the disciples of the Lord saw and heard in the Garden of Gethsemane, for unfortunately, they slept most of the night. Had they remained awake, more might have been known of the sufferings of the Lord. There exists the possibility that between the periods of slumber they witnessed some of the things described in the Gospels, or perhaps another disciple entered the garden and saw what was later described to the writers of the synoptic records. It is impossible to instruct sleeping people. There are times when it is wiser not to sleep. Luke wrote: ". . . when they were awake, they saw his glory" (see Luke 9:32). Unfortunately, there were times in the history of the church when Christians suffered from sleeping sickness. When the drowsiness terminated and the assemblies awakened, the revival which followed indicated a new vision of the glorified Christ had transformed the followers of the Savior.

It appears to be significant that Mark wrote: "And they came to a place which was named Gethsemane, and he saith to his disciples sit ye here while I shall pray. And he taketh with him Peter and James and John, and began to be sore amazed and to be very heavy" (overwhelmed with anguish). Adam Clark, the noted commentator, says: "The word is used by the Greeks to describe the most extreme anguish which the soul can feel; excruciating anxiety, and torture of spirit." The other disciples cannot be blamed for their absence; they were obeying their Master, Who ordered them to remain outside of the garden. That three disciples were permitted to accompany Him indicated He desired their presence. They had witnessed His glory in the mountain, and were now to see His sufferings in the garden. The Lion of the tribe of Judah was to be viewed as the Lamb of God. The other disciples may have thought they were to act as guards; to give warning of approaching danger. This was the third occasion when these special men were permitted to witness the unusual. They saw His glory in the mountain, His greatness when the daughter of Jairus was restored to life, and His grace in the garden where the kindness of the Lord was manifested to every person present. He could have summoned an army of angels, but did not. He could have destroyed His enemies, but refused to do so. The poet was correct when he wrote: "What a wonderful Savior is Jesus my Lord." See the later chapter which described Simon Peter's actions in Gethsemane.

11

PETER TELLS THE LORD
NOT TO BE FOOLISH

"And Jesus said, Who touched me? And when all denied, Peter and they that were with him said: Master, the multitude throng thee and press thee, and sayest thou, Who touched me? And Jesus said, Somebody hath touched me: for I perceive that virtue is gone out of me? (Luke 8:45–46).

The street was crowded with people but although many were excited, others were frowning. The unbelievable had taken place; the impossible had happened. The respected and revered ruler of the synagogue had made a spectacle of himself by seeking the help of Jesus whom he had formerly condemned. His daughter of twelve years was seriously ill, and some critics were debating who or what should have priority in the father's thoughts—his girl, or his allegiance to the prestige of the synagogue. It was easy for the onlookers to pass judgment; their children were not dying. Peter's eyes shone with excitement and when the Master consented to go with the distraught parent, the disciples were elated. This would be a day to be remembered.

Then suddenly the procession was unexpectedly brought to a halt. As the Lord was pushing His way through the crowd, He stopped and asked: "Who touched me?" The people nearest to Him momentarily felt guilty as though they had invaded the Lord's privacy. Simon Peter then said: "Master, that is a strange thing to ask. Look at this huge crowd. It is hardly possible to get through the street. In the last ten yards dozens of people have touched You. Even if they only brushed against You, they at least touched You." That question is strange considering the circumstances.

"And Jesus said, Somebody hath touched me; for I perceive that virtue is gone out of me. And when the woman saw that she was not hid, she came trembling, and falling down before him, she declared unto him before all the people for what cause she had touched him, and how she was healed immediately. And he said unto her: Daughter, be of good comfort; thy faith hath made thee whole; go in peace" (Luke 8:46–48).

"Momentarily the scene beggared description for the crowds were so large that it was hard to make progress. *The Amplified Testament* renders the foregoing passage: 'As Jesus went, the people pressed around him—*almost suffocating Him.*' Therefore it follows that within the space of a few yards many people had touched Him. He was in the position of having to force a way through the crowds. It was for this very reason that the disciples were probably dumbfounded when the Lord asked, 'Who touched Me?' The woman's touch might have been unnoticed; but her faith gripped His heart. It was the magnetic quality of her sincere desire which drew from His boundless resources the healing she desperately needed. He felt virtue going out of Him; someone's need was being met; His life was being drained to help another; He was giving a spiritual blood transfusion in a very real way, and since this could not happen by chance, there had to be a cause.

"Could He who knew so much be ignorant of the woman's identity? Did He ask His question because He did not know who touched Him? Did He ask in order to help her come out into the open to make her first unashamed confession of faith? There would be people in that crowd who knew her condition. She was unclean, but even of more consequence was the fact that she was contaminating other people. Unless this woman's case be publicized, there could be serious repercussions. It would not be safe to let her go away unnoticed, for someone might have seen her, and that someone might inform the authorities. The Lord's action was kindness in disguise" (quoted from the author's commentary, *Luke's Thrilling Gospel*, Kregel Publications, Grand Rapids, Michigan).

One wonders what effect this had upon Simon Peter who had questioned the Lord's earlier statement. Probably he wished he had remained silent. However, it was an ill wind that blew no good; the hasty disciple learned from his experience.

Peter Recognized the Lord's Wisdom

Simon Peter was self-assertive; he never lacked confidence, and often "rushed in where angels feared to tread." Consequently, anything which did not gain his immediate approval was suspect. He needed to learn that God's ways were not always desired by men; even unpleasant events could be arranged by the Almighty, and trust in a heavenly Father was more to be desired than a life of ease. As Christ knew about the impoverished woman, He also knew about Peter and all His followers. The poet was correct when he wrote: "God moves in a mysterious way, His wonders to perform! He plants His footsteps in the sea, and rides upon the storm."

Peter Respected the Lord's Willingness

The woman who touched the fringe of His garment was an outcast despised by everybody. Even the doctors ignored her when she had no more money to pay for their services. Peter and the disciples must have been astounded when the Lord treated her favorably.

F. L. Godet quotes Eusebius as saying this woman was a heathen and dwelt at Paneas, near the source of the Jordan, and that in his time her house was still shown, having at its entrance two brass statues on a stone pedestal. One represented a woman on her knees, with her hands held out before her, in the attitude of a suppliant; the other, a man standing with his cloak thrown over his shoulder, and his hand extended toward the woman. Eusebius had been into the house himself, and had seen this statue, which represented, it was said, the features of Jesus (*Godet on John*, p. 393). It is difficult to estimate how much reliability may be placed on this statement handed down from a bygone age. One thing remains indisputable; this woman was in an unenviable position. Over a period of twelve years she had suffered from recurring hemorrhages, and her continuing visits to the physicians had impoverished her beyond measure. The fifteenth chapter of the book of Leviticus has much to say of a woman in this condition. She was not only considered to be unclean herself; she also defiled anyone or anything she touched. If she were a Jewess, she would be an unfortunate woman with whom no one would wish to associate. The fact that her condition had continued over a period of twelve years would suggest this was a judgment from God. If she were a Gentile, a heathen, as Eusebius suggests, then she would be even more unclean in the estimation of her Jewish neighbors. Thus, viewed from any angle, this woman was an object of pity; a desolate, dejected case for whom the physicians could do nothing.

Peter Responded to the Lord's Work

It is interesting to discover that the messenger who came to inform Jairus about the death of his daughter, referred to Jesus as THE MASTER. Did that signify that as there were saints in the household of Caesar, there were believers among the ruler's family and friends? Is it possible that this unnamed disciple had been responsible for the action of the distressed parent? The answers to these questions are not easily obtained, but Simon Peter was present when these events took place. He and his comrades were filled with expectation. When they approached the home and heard the cries of the professional mourners, their wailing was so hypocritical the Savior ordered their dismissal. The Lord could not tolerate such false exhibitionism. Jesus invited Peter, James and John to accompany Him to the room where the girl's body lay upon a bed. He was calm when He said: "Little girl, wake up." Peter heard the Master saying to the parents: "Don't cry! She is not dead, but sleepeth." Then, a tremor slightly moved the eyelids; a flush began to appear on the child's face, and finally her eyes opened and she was quickly embraced by her mother. Simon wanted to rush to the housetop to publicize the amazing miracle, but the Lord said: "Don't tell a soul. No matter what people say, just smile and remain silent. That will prevent a lot of argument and strife. And by the way, your girl needs food." Peter probably smiled— the Master thought of everything!

12

WET IN A HURRY

"And Peter answered him and said, Lord, if it be thou, bid me come unto thee on the water. And he said, Come. And when Peter was come down out of the ship, he walked on the water to go to Jesus. But when he saw the wind boisterous, he was afraid, and beginning to sink, he cried saying, Lord, save me. And immediately, Jesus stretched forth his hand, and caught him, and said unto him, O thou of little faith, wherefore didst thou doubt?" (Matthew 14:28–31).

It seems strange that this remarkable experience of Simon Peter was only mentioned by Matthew. The storm which preceded it was mentioned by all the other Gospel writers, but for some inscrutable reason, Mark, Luke and John omitted to describe this event. Mark, who was Simon's secretary, never spoke about his friend's walk on the water. Either he did not wish to publicize what he did, or Mark did not desire to write about an action which many people would consider to be stupid.

An Impulsive Request

"And Peter answered him and said, Lord, if it be thou, bid me come unto thee on the water" (Matthew 14:28).

Apparently, Peter was on cloud nine! When the Lord miraculously fed the hungry multitude, the disciples had reveled in the amazing ability of their Lord. They would have joyfully participated in a premature coronation. John wrote: "When Jesus therefore perceived that they would come and take him by force, to make him a king, he departed again into a mountain himself alone" (John 6:15). The disciples, who had arranged for the crowd to be seated in groups of fifty, were ready and willing to act in a similar fashion to organize men into regiments to fight on behalf of their Champion. The Savior recognized the danger of such actions, and ordered His friends to sail across the sea toward Capernaum. Afterward, He dispersed the crowd and climbed the hillside to pray. The men needed, temporarily at least, to think about other matters.

Jesus was probably aware of the approach of a storm, and deliberately sent His friends into it. A few hours of hard work would be helpful. During the rest of the night and into the early hours of the morning, He watched as they struggled to survive. About three o'clock in the morning He came unto them walking on the water. The disciples cried out in fear, believing a ghost was about to increase their problems. Then they heard Jesus saying, "It is I, be not afraid." Suddenly, Simon Peter, who was already agitated, said: "Lord, if it be Thou, bid me come unto thee on the water." That utterance was possibly one of the strangest requests ever made by the impulsive fisherman. When Satan suggested a similar thing to the Lord, he was rebuked:

> "And Jesus answering said unto him, It is said, Thou shalt not tempt the Lord thy God" (Luke 4:12).

When God gave intelligence to man, He expected it to be used. The Savior did so; His disciple did not.

It might be argued that the Lord gave permission for Simon to leave the boat, and the disciple was therefore justified in his action. It should be remembered that the Savior can make even our mistakes to become a source of instruction. If Christ cared for us only when we were blameless, He would have a lot of time to spare.

An Immense Realization

> "But when he saw the wind boisterous, he was afraid; and beginning to sink, he cried, saying, Lord, save me" (Matthew 14:30).

Peter's enthusiasm was quickly destroyed. He should have known better! When he became terrified the consequences of his rash action seemed to be appalling. As he was about to disappear beneath the waves, his short, desperate prayer probably brought a smile to the Savior's face. His cry was spontaneous, simple, and sufficient. The impulsive disciple learned a great lesson that day, but it did not change his impetuosity. He continued to make similar mistakes.

"But when he saw the wind boisterous." The *Amplified New Testament* renders this passage, "But when he perceived, and felt the strong wind, he was frightened." This was always Peter's weakness. He denied his Lord at the fire because he ceased watching the Master to see a girl. He asked a foolish question on the beach of the Sea of Galilee because he saw John, not Jesus. He was later rebuked by Paul because once again he became more anxious to please Jewish observers than to adhere to the precepts of the new faith (see Galatians 2:11–13). Charles Alexander, the famous gospel singer, sang at a school for the blind. At the end of his performance, he offered to sing anyone's favorite hymn. A blind boy lifted his hand and said, "Please, Sir, sing 'Never Lose Sight of Jesus.'" That blind child had excellent vision!" (Copied from *Matthew's Majestic Gospel*, Kregel Publications, Grand Rapids, Michigan.)

One wonders what might have happened to Simon Peter had he neglected to pray. Probably the Lord would have rescued him, but in any situation it pays to pray! This is a lesson all people need to learn. Jesus could not leave him to drown! Peter made many errors, but he was never abandoned. It is refreshing to know that Christ still walks on the sea of life searching for men in need. Even the noise of a storm cannot prevent the Lord from hearing whispers.

Many years ago I visited the marvelous cathedrals in Italy, and in one, saw a woman painfully proceeding on her bare knees the entire length of the church. She was performing this painful act to obtain the forgiveness of her sins. A week later, I saw the same woman doing the same thing in another cathedral. When I asked an attendant about her, he smiled, and said: "Oh, we all know her. She visits all the cathedrals of Italy and hopes by her actions to obtain forgiveness for her sins." I wanted to inform her there was no need to crawl through churches, for pardon is the free gift of God made possible through the death of the Savior. The poor lady who was apparently threatened by a storm of guilt, was unaware of the good news found in the Gospel.

Simon Peter's prayer consisted of three words, but the first was the most important. He cried saying, "Lord, save me." The Bible says that "no man can say that Jesus is Lord but by the Holy Ghost" (1 Corinthians 12:3). Jonah was safe in a fish under the sea; Peter was rescued in the sea; and when he returned with Christ was safe on the sea. In any place and age it pays to be a friend of the Lord. When Peter was in danger, his cry for assistance brought an immediate response. Probably he had been drenched many times during his fishing career, but when he saw the outstretched hand of the Savior, he probably held on with both hands and whispered, "Lord, don't let me go." That troubled disciple needed to learn that nothing could separate him from the love of Christ. Paul was correct when he wrote:

"For I am persuaded, that neither death, nor life, nor angels, nor principalities, nor powers, nor things present, nor things to come. Nor height, nor depth, nor any other creature, shall be able to separate us from the love of God, which is in Christ Jesus our Lord" (Romans 8:38–39).

An Important Remark

It is important to remember that Simon walked on the water a second time when he accompanied the Savior back to the boat. Through the power imparted by the Master, he trampled under foot the waves which might have ended his life. This could not have been done in his own strength, but with Paul he could say: "I can do all things through Christ which strengtheneth me" (see Philippians 4:13).

"They . . . worshipped him, saying, Of a truth thou art the Son of God." Those disciples were wet, scared, tired and amazed. They had witnessed the impossible; even the storm had subsided; the wind and waves no longer threatened their existence. Obviously, no man could have accomplished what their Master had done. Even the weather was subject to His control. He must be; He had to be the Son of the living God. The boat was now completely still; the lake had become a mill pond. Calmly, the Lord of creation sat in the stern of the boat; a boat which had become a holy place. Slowly, the men, one by one, knelt at His feet; *they worshipped him*. Blessed are they who worship in the sanctuary, but even more thrilled are the people who can find and *worship* Him anywhere.

> What matters where on earth we dwell:
> On mountain top or in the dell?
> In cottage or a mansion fair,
> Where Jesus is, 'tis heaven there.

(Reprinted from the author's commentary, *Matthew's Majestic Gospel,* Kregel Publications, Grand Rapids, Michigan.)

Peter ... *Whose Ardor Was Somewhat Dampened*

Simon Peter did many praiseworthy things during the course of his lifetime, but this episode of walking upon the water must rank as one of the greatest. When fear had frayed his nervous energies, and when a seeming apparition had startled the entire crew, the realization that the Savior had drawn near was a little too much for Peter's self-control. In the excitement and relief of the moment he cried, "Lord, if it be thou, bid me come unto thee on the water. And Jesus said, Come. And when Peter was come down out of the ship, he walked on the water, to go to Jesus."

A Triumphant Response

We must never underestimate the greatness of Peter's achievement. Surrounded by obvious dangers and faced with utter impossibilities, he found strength in his Lord's command; and forgetting all else, stepped into the midst of a noisy tempest. *And he did not sink.* It seems fitting that this should have happened to Peter, for in later days he was destined to be the evangelist of the Church. Few pictures could so aptly reveal the beginning of a Christian journey. When Christ draws near to the tempest-tossed souls of men and women, the sound of His voice brings life's greatest challenge. Eventually the soul is confronted by the call to leave a comparatively safe boat in order to step into the unknown. Reason and doubt would shrink from this; but a burning heart, an eager soul, and a waiting Christ are very hard to deny.

A Terrible Reality

The story presents no difficulties to the man who has responded to a similar invitation. The facts of Christian experience prove that no man was ever engulfed by temptation while he steadfastly looked at his Savior. Through His enabling grace, it is possible to trample under foot the very waves that would bury us. Yet, even the greatest saint is endangered when he loses sight of his Lord. "But when Peter saw the wind boisterous, he was afraid; and beginning to sink . . . " Frantic despair gripped the sinking man as he cried, "Lord, save me." Possibly he thought he had been unwise to leave the boat; but in later years saner judgment admitted that the mistake lay in losing sight of his Lord. When he ceased listening to and looking at his Master, dangers overcame him.

A Trembling Request

Peter's prayer is one of the best on record. There are no superfluous words, and no unnecessary finesse of phraseology. It is the quickest, easiest, and most desperate way of reaching the heart of God. "Lord, save me." His sudden cry reveals three vital things. (1) *His predicament.* He was sinking, and every moment counted if he were to be saved from drowning. (2) *His perception.* Christ was near, and was able to save. The ability of the Master more than equaled the demands of the moment. If only He *would*, He *could* meet Peter's need. (3) *His prayer.* There was no time to elaborate any details, and no time to observe any ceremonial law. One thing mattered, and that was to be saved. It banished all else from Peter's mind, and he cried, "Lord, save me." This modern world would be well advised to emulate Peter's example.

A Timely Reply

"'And immediately Jesus stretched forth his hand and caught him, and said unto him, O thou of little faith, wherefore didst thou doubt?' The surging waves gave up their victim, and as Peter instinctively wiped the water from his eyes, he realized that once again he was standing on the sea. The boat was some distance away, but fear had now disappeared. A new calm had settled upon his mind, for he was conscious that Christ still held his hand. His clothing was saturated with water, but every moment, increasing elation drove the chill from his spirits. Yes, he could walk on the water that would have drowned him. Maybe in after years Paul gave to Peter a text to fit the occasion. 'I can do all things through Christ which strengtheneth me' (Philippians 4:13). The secret of every Christian triumph seems to be expressed in the two words: *'through Christ.'*

> Hold thou my hand: so weak I am and helpless;
> I dare not go one step without Thy aid.
> Hold Thou my hand: for then, O loving Savior,
> No dread of ill shall make my soul afraid."

(Reprinted from the author's book, *Bible Pinnacles*, Kregel Publications, Grand Rapids, Michigan.)

13

CHOSEN FOR A SPECIAL ASSIGNMENT

---

*"And when they were come nigh to Jerusalem, unto Bethphage
and Bethany, at the mount of Olives, he sendeth forth two of his
disciples" (Mark 11:1).*

There were occasions during the ministry of the Lord when it
became necessary to make arrangements for forthcoming events.
When Jesus was about to enter Jerusalem, He sent two of His disciples to bring the donkey upon which His special entry was to be
made. Describing that incident Matthew said He commissioned two
of His friends to perform that task (see Matthew 21:2). Mark wrote:
"He sendeth forth two of his disciples" (Mark 11:1), and Luke supplied similar information (see Luke 19:20–30). It is intriguing to
note that none of these writers identified the men by name. Nevertheless, other theologians expressed certain ideas. Bede believed they
were Simon and Philip; and some eminent teachers believed them to
be Simon and John. This appears to have more credibility for when
two disciples were sent to arrange for the Passover, they were identified as Peter and John (see Luke 22:8). When all the evidence is
considered it seems reasonable to believe that the two fishermen who
had been with Him since the beginning of His ministry were given
the privilege of representing their Master.

The Previous Arrangement ... *Peter's Instruction*

At the Passover Jerusalem was always overcrowded, for according to ancient records, three million attended the celebration. It was
exceedingly difficult to obtain accommodation, and last-minute arrangements were impossible to make. Jesus was aware of the situation, and on an earlier visit discussed the matter with one of His
friends. Every detail was planned and, to prevent the stealing of the
animals, a password was chosen by which the identity of the autho-
rized messengers would be established.

"Dr. William Barclay also thinks this had been prearranged by the Lord during an earlier visit to the city. The Lord had many friends in the neighborhood, and if Barclay's suggestion is correct, then Jesus had privately warned one of them of what eventually would take place. The man was willing to help in any way possible, but to prevent his animal from being stolen, chose a password by which the identity of the men to be sent would be recognized. 'The Lord hath need of him,' the words quoted in all the synoptic versions must have been prearranged between Jesus and that unknown friend. The site of Bethany is well known, but the place and importance of Bethphage are obscure. It has been said that Bethphage was a suburb of Jerusalem; that it was a convenient extension to the sacred precincts of the city; an extension made necessary by the ever-increasing numbers of pilgrims who came to the feasts. There were legal requirements which demanded that worshippers should be housed within the camp—the city, but when this became an impossibility, something had to be done to remedy the situation. The priests therefore, or so it has been claimed, *sanctified* that portion of land which stretched out from the city walls toward the Mount of Olives. This was known as Bethphage. Bethany itself was only two miles from Jerusalem, and therefore it should be easily understood why the two places appear together in the sacred record. It has been estimated from ancient records that the number of people attending this feast would have been in excess of three million, and Jerusalem was unable to accommodate that number. Hence, many of the pilgrims would need housing outside the immediate city, and it was for that reason the priests *sanctified* the additional territory.

"To appreciate the full significance of Christ's entry into the city, it is necessary to visualize what was taking place. Many pilgrims were already there, and every street was crowded to capacity. People had traveled great distances, and probably had heard strange and wonderful stories about the new Prophet. Naturally, they would wish to see Him if that were possible. The city itself had put on its finery; shopkeepers were eager for trade, and possibly flags were flying everywhere. This had always been the greatest event in the year, and the present feast promised to surpass anything ever known. It was common knowledge that the Scribes and Pharisees were determined to accuse the Prophet, and at least imprison Him. It was freely said in the market place that plans had been made whereby He might even be crucified. To say the least, the future promised to be exciting!"

(Quoted from the author's commentary, *Luke's Thrilling Gospel*, Kregel Publishing Company, Grand Rapids, Michigan.)

The Proud Animal . . . *Peter's Interest*

Simon Peter may not have been too enthusiastic about his mission for the Lord had stated the donkey had never been tamed. An unbroken colt can be a nightmare to any rider. Its arching back, twisting, rebellious sides, and kicking feet can present problems hard to solve. An inexperienced rider may land in the dust. Skilled in the art of breaking animals, cowboys can subdue such beasts, but even they have to tame unruly steeds. It was significant that the unbroken colt upon which Christ entered the city was never rebellious; he never put up a fight.

It might be important to remember that authority over all animals was given to the first human (see Genesis 1:28), but this was forfeited when man disobeyed God's commandment and became a sinner. The Savior had the same ability, and that explained why the unbroken colt was so docile. Adam's error produced many problems from which his descendants have continuously suffered. It is refreshing to know that the day is approaching when the lion will lie down with the lamb, and nothing shall hurt in all God's holy mountain (see Isaiah 11:9).

The Potent Announcement . . . *Peter's Inspiration*

"All this was done that it might be fulfilled which was spoken by the prophet saying: Tell ye the daughter of Zion, Behold, thy king cometh unto thee, meek, and sitting upon an ass, and a colt, the foal of an ass" (Matthew 21:4–5; see also Zechariah 9:9).

Simon Peter was surely impressed with the accuracy of the Lord's instructions. Jesus described where and how the colt could be found. He had told precisely at which house the animal would be found, and even the presence of people who would question the disciples' actions. Evidently Jesus and His unknown friend had arranged everything even to the password which would quell the fears of neighbors. There was reason to believe that Peter was aware of the statement made by the prophet Zechariah. That prediction had often been read in the synagogue where he had been an attentive listener. This became evident on the day of Pentecost when his sermon referred to various statements made by the prophets.

This action of the Lord registered a definite change in His ministry. He had told demons and men to hold their peace, and refrain from publicizing information which would encourage criticism and opposition. Now everything had changed; nothing was to be done secretly. The disciples recognized the significance of this noisy entrance into the city, and when the crowd began chanting, excitement filled the streets; they believed the long desired kingdom was about to be established. Peter was elated, and even the proud little donkey seemed to be enjoying the occasion.

The Public Acclamation . . . *Peter's Involvement*

"And when he was come nigh, even now at the descent of the mount of Olives, the whole multitude of the disciples, began to rejoice and praise God with a loud voice for all the mighty works that they had seen. Saying, Blessed be the King that cometh in the name of the Lord; peace in heaven and glory in the highest" (Luke 19:37–38).

It would be very difficult to express all that Simon Peter felt on that memorable day. The loss of his fishing business and separation from family and friends seemed unimportant when compared with the happiness within his soul. The emotional outburst from the tremendous crowds repaid any loss which he had sustained. Doubt, which may have occurred, was instantly dispatched, for he was thrilled with the privilege of accompanying his Master into the city. Even the donkey seemed to appreciate what was taking place. It seemed strange that this animal should permit the King of Kings to ride upon its back when the leaders of the nation opposed everything Jesus did. Sometimes even donkeys are wiser than men. Balaam, the compromising prophet, discovered that fact when the ass rebuked the foolishness of its master (see Numbers 23:28). The Lord did not respond to the plaudits of the multitude, and later when He looked at the city, He wept.

It should be remembered that the Gospels were written many years later, and the order in which the events took place seems confusing. Luke seems to infer that the Lord went immediately to Jerusalem. The other Gospels indicate that after the triumphant entry, Jesus returned to stay the night in Bethany. The following morning, as He returned to Jerusalem, He saw the fruitless fig tree. Simon Peter was disappointed and devastated by the Lord's reaction. When he saw the Savior's tears and dwindling crowds, all chance of establishing the kingdom of Christ vanished. He believed that if the Lord had given encouragement to the people, the Roman invaders might have been expelled. He probably sighed and whispered: "Oh, Lord, did you have to weep?" To their everlasting credit it may be said that when the people began to leave, the disciples remained. As Simon had previously said, "Unto whom can we go? Thou hast the words of eternal life."

The followers of Christ had much to learn. Had the Lord encouraged the enthusiastic multitude, insurrection would have spread through the city, and the arrival of Roman soldiers might have led to a massacre. Jesus desired peace, but for a time at least, the disciples failed to understand that fact. After the Savior had wept over the city, they probably wondered what might have happened had the Lord's behavior been different. The only happiness which remained undiminished belonged to the young donkey feeding in his stall. He had carried the Lord of Creation, and that fact probably made ordinary food taste like a king's banquet!

14

PETER PUT TWO AND TWO TOGETHER

"And on the morrow, when they were come from Bethany, he was hungry, and seeing a fig tree afar off having leaves, he came, if haply he might find anything thereon; and when he came to it, he found nothing but leaves; for the time of figs was not yet. And Jesus answered and said unto it, No man eat of fruit of thee hereafter forever. And his disciples heard it . . . And in the morning, as they passed by, they saw the fig tree dried up from the roots. And Peter calling to remembrance saith unto him, Master, behold the fig tree which thou cursedst is withered away. And Jesus answering saith unto them, Have faith in God" (Mark 11:12–14 and 20–22).

Mark said that after Christ's entry into Jerusalem, the Lord returned to Bethany where in all probability, He visited friends and enjoyed a meal in the home of Simon. Afterward, the night was spent in solitude as He prepared for His approaching ordeal. The following morning as He walked toward Jerusalem, He became hungry. It is difficult to believe that the night had been spent in the home of Martha, for she would not have permitted His leaving without breakfast. Possibly the Savior instructed the gracious hostess that He would not require the early meal as He planned to leave soon after sunrise. As the Lord proceeded on His way, He saw what was apparently a flourishing fig tree, but unfortunately, it had only leaves. Evidently He was disappointed and to the astonishment of the disciples, pronounced a curse upon it. Mark stated "the time of figs was not yet" (see Mark 11:13). Unwise people have criticized the Lord for punishing a tree for not bearing out-of-season fruit.

"In the East the fig tree produces two definite crops of figs per season. The normal winter figs ripen in May and June, and the summer figs in August and September. Sometimes the crops overlap. The baby fig buds are generally seen in February before the leaves appear in April each year. It is possible to pick figs over nine or ten months of the year in Israel . . . Our Lord condemned the fig tree at Passover time (April). This tree should have borne early, ripe figs. The Lord would have known whether the tree should have been cropping. Moses had said that fruit on trees by the wayside could be picked by passersby. A fig tree produces masses of large green leaves and gives ample welcome shade in a hot country" (W. E. Shewell-Cooper, *The Zondervan Pictorial Encyclopedia of the Bible*, vol. 2, p. 534).

"This fig tree had leaves, but no fruit, for it was not the season of fruit. Other trees would be bare at this early season, but the fig trees would be putting forth their broad green leaves. It is possible that this tree, standing by itself as it would seem, was more forward than the other trees around. It was seen from afar and therefore it must have had the full benefit of the sun . . . But then it is peculiar to the fig tree that its fruit begins to appear before its leaves. It was therefore a natural supposition that on this tree, with its leaves fully developed, there might be found at least some ripened fruit . . . The leaves of this fig tree deceived the passerby, who, from seeing them, would naturally expect the fruit. And so the fig tree was cursed, not for being barren, but for being false" (*The Pulpit Commentary, Mark*, p. 121). The statement "for the time of figs was not yet" can only mean "for the time of fruit-gathering, or the time of harvest, was not yet." It will be seen therefore that criticism of this incident was unjust and uninformed" (quoted from the author's commentary, *Mark's Superb Gospel*, Kregel Publications, Grand Rapids, Michigan).

It seems the significance of the cursing of the barren fig tree did not impress the disciples until the following day when it became evident the disaster was unprecedented. The tree had died from the roots upward. When trees or plants die, death begins with the leaves and branches, but in this case, disaster had spread upward from the roots as if the soil itself had been contaminated. As usual, it was Simon Peter who drew attention to the calamity. He said, "Master, behold the fig tree which thou cursedst is withered away." He recalled what had happened on the previous day, and as men now say, he put two and two together and reached certain conclusions. He probably knew that the Lord detested falsehood and hypocrisy; for He had expelled moneychangers from the temple and rebuked Pharisees who taught one thing and practiced another.

The fig tree had often been used by the prophets as a symbol of the prosperity of the Hebrew nation (see 1 Kings 4:25 and Micah 4:4). Figs were made into cakes and some of these were brought to David (see 1 Chronicles 12:40). Abigail, on another occasion, brought two hundred cakes of figs to David in Hebron (see 1 Samuel 25:18). Possibly Simon Peter was aware of these events, and the death of the fig tree became significant.

A Solemn Warning ... *Fear*

The disciple surely realized the incident constituted a warning to those whose lives were barren. An old Greek maxim said that man's chief end is to glorify God. Unfortunately, there were, and still are, many people in whom the fruit of the Holy Spirit is never found; their profession is misleading; they produce "nothing but leaves." Under law retribution was inevitable, but forgiving grace made a tremendous difference. That explanation appears to be the only logical interpretation of the Lord's reply to Simon Peter. It was obvious that Jesus expected to find fruit on a tree which had become unproductive; it no longer justified its existence. The fact that it stood alone may suggest it received more sunshine than the others, and therefore could be expected to bear early fruit. The man who planted the tree had labored in vain.

Since the fig tree had been compared with the Hebrew nation, it is not difficult to understand why God expected so much from His chosen people; they were the "apple of His eye," and had been specially favored throughout their history. Their shallow profession of sincerity had been detestable in the sight of Jehovah, Who had supplied much only to receive nothing in return. The luxuriant leaves only hid the absence of fruit. Instead of supplying food for the hungry, it remained fruitless. That distressing incident should be a warning to people whose actions contradict their testimony.

The Spiritual Wisdom ... *Faith*

Peter was surely surprised when in response to his statement, the Savior replied: "Have faith in God." If he expected an explanation why the tree had died, he was disappointed. He had no desire to destroy trees, and to speak about the necessity of possessing great faith seemed irrelevant. Nevertheless, the Lord's remark gained Peter's attention. When Jesus proceeded to speak about removing a mountain into the sea, the statement appeared to be confusing. At that time the Savior was standing on the Mount of Olives, and Peter's thoughts

82

immediately envisaged faith moving the hill to the Mediterranean Sea, which was impossible. Bulldozers may move a great quantity of earth, but no man ever used faith to relocate a mountain.

Evidently the Lord was considering other mountains, such as problems hard to solve. Many difficulties lay ahead of His followers; there would be occasions when they would not know what to do. Reason would fail, friends disappear, and the outlook be exceptionally bleak. Their greatest asset would be prayer, which unlocked Heaven's treasure house. Jesus said: "Therefore I say unto you, What things soever ye desire, when ye pray believe that ye receive them, and ye shall have them" (Mark 11:24). Doubt causes spiritual paralysis. Yet anything is possible when Christians truly believe. Yet it must be admitted when great difficulties impede progress, it is not easy to remove "them into the midst of the sea." Sometimes people ask for assistance but their prayers remain unanswered, and fear eclipses faith.

It is wise to remember that true prayer coincides with the will of God. At creation the Lord placed the Mount of Olives in its location, and had it been necessary He could have changed its position. The Savior can also remove our problems, but there are times when instead of removing the mountain, He supplies strength to climb it. To succeed in accomplishing a difficult task is often more rewarding than easy victories. It is always helpful to remember that we have a Guide Who helps in every emergency.

A Sincere Winsomeness . . . *Fellowship*

It was truly thought-provoking when the Lord changed the topic of His conversation. He said:

> "And when ye stand praying, forgive, if ye have ought against any; that your Father also which is in heaven may forgive you your trespasses. But if he do not forgive, neither will your Father which is in heaven forgive your trespasses" (Mark 11:25–26).

When the Savior emphasized the necessity of forgiveness He indicated that compassion is more important than apparent miracles. If a person permits bitterness to dominate his soul, prayer becomes ineffective, and mountains never move. Anything is possible, but nothing can be expected unless compassion fills the soul of the supplicant. It must be remembered that God will not forgive us unless

83

we exhibit the same love toward our neighbor. Prayer is a waste of time unless men and women are compassionate. Paul wrote to his friends urging them to "forgive one another even as God for Christ's sake hath forgiven you" (Ephesians 4:23). Like the fig tree we disappointed Christ many times, but He was merciful. We must emulate His example.

15

A LAMB THAT WAS NEVER USED

"Now the first day of the feast of unleavened bread the disciples came to Jesus, saying, Where wilt thou that we prepare for thee to eat the Passover? And he said, Go into the city to such a man, and say unto him, the Master saith, My time is at hand; I will keep the Passover at thy house with my disciples. And the disciples did as Jesus had appointed them; and they made ready the Passover" (Matthew 26:17–19).

The Feast of Unleavened Bread, otherwise known as the Passover, was the most important event in the Hebrew calendar; attendance for all males was mandatory. Crowds of people came from many countries, but even those who could not make the journey, celebrated the feast either in their homes or communities. The Lord had probably arranged with a friend that a special room in his house be available where the disciples could honor the occasion. To make last-minute arrangements would have been futile, for upward of three million visitors would be coming to Jerusalem. It was interesting that for the first time James was not included with Peter and John who were given precise instructions regarding the assignment. They were to enter the city and look for a man carrying a pitcher of water. This was most unusual for that task was usually performed by women. It would be beyond reason to see two men performing that act at the identical time and place. When Peter and John saw a man carrying water, they followed him until they reached a large home where they met its owner, and said: "The Master says, My time is at hand; I will keep the Passover at thy house with my disciples" (Luke 22:10–12).

It has been suggested that this home belonged to the parents of John Mark, and that it became a meeting place for the apostles (compare Acts 12:12). This might have been true, for a large house owned by followers of Jesus would have been hard to find in that hostile city. The owner had gone to great lengths to prepare for his guests. A

85

large upper room had been furnished; additional couches or recliners had been carried up the stairs, for at least thirteen men would be celebrating. Plates, a large table, and other utensils would be needed. The man explained what had been provided and then withdrew, leaving the two disciples to complete their preparation.

"They provided unfermented bread, wine, bitter herbs, sauce, and some dishes necessary for the feast. They would not eat the Paschal lamb at the legal time tomorrow, so the Lord ordained a commemorative and anticipatory solemnity in which he appointed a rite which should take the place of the Jewish ceremony. We learn from the other synoptists that the householder was not satisfied with offering Christ and his friends the use of the common hall which they would have had to share probably with other guests, but he assigned to them his best and most honorable chamber, 'a large upper room' already properly arranged and furnished for the feast. Tradition has maintained that this apartment was afterwards used by the apostles as a place of assembling, and where they received the effusion of the Holy Ghost on the Day of Pentecost" (*Pulpit Commentary*, Wm. B. Eerdmans Publishing Co., Grand Rapids, Michigan).

It is important to remember that unless Peter and John had been explicitly instructed not to provide a lamb, the securing of a sacrifice would have been their most important task. There had never been a Passover without a sacrifice. The father of John Mark might have foreseen the need, and his thoughtfulness may have simplified the task of the disciples. Peter and John would have known that without a lamb of the first year, it would have been impossible to observe the Passover. If arrangements were made according to the usual procedure, the animal was purchased, examined and certified by a priest in the temple, and then placed in readiness for the moment when it would be slain. When the Lord arrived with the disciples, everything was in readiness for the celebration.

"And when the Lord was come, he sat down and his twelve apostles with him."

Apparently, this was the first time in history when a Passover was observed without a lamb, the shedding of blood, and at which no meat was consumed. Certain features invite investigation.

The Strange Mystery ... *Surprising*

Was Simon Peter filled with questions as he watched the celebrations proceeding? During his lifetime he had attended many feasts, and knew the order of service. As the head of a household he might have presided over such functions himself, and knew what to expect next. When the moment approached for worshipers to eat the roasted lamb, did he stare at the Savior and anticipate difficulties? When Paul wrote to the Colossians he said:

" . . . the mystery which hath been hid from ages and from generations, but now is made manifest to the saints. To whom God would make known what is the riches of the glory of this mystery among the Gentiles, which is Christ in you, the hope of glory" (Colossians 1:26–27).

To the disciples was given the privilege of witnessing the most profound transition in history. Something planned before the commencement of time actually took place in their presence; God's plans were being fulfilled. What had been restricted boundaries for one favored nation was being immeasurably enlarged to include the human race. All people were to be given the opportunity of becoming the children of God. The Passover, which was so valued by the Hebrews, was to be followed by another feast at which all believers could partake of the Bread of Life. Millions of sacrifices would soon be replaced by the Lamb of God whose precious blood would become a ransom for many. If Simon Peter sought answers to his questions, they were quickly forthcoming. The Lord seemed to be saying: "Are you expecting a lamb? Then look at Me, for I am the Lamb of God which taketh away the sins of the world. This bread is as my body; and this wine as my blood which is shed for the remission of sin. Eat, drink, and live. Behold I set before you an open door. Arise and enter."

The Stately Master ... *Serene*

" . . . and Jesus took bread, and blessed it, and brake it, and gave it to the disciples, and said: Take, eat; this is my body" (Matthew 26:26).

The large upper room was very quiet; the world far away! The clamor of the excited crowds, and the requests of suffering people forgotten. The disciples were watching their Master. A wonderful peace seemed to be reflected in His eyes as He took the bread from the table and quietly said: "This is my body." No one moved; no sound was heard. Peter was probably fascinated, and John was reminiscing. Deep within his soul he was beginning to suspect what later he wrote in his Gospel. "In the beginning was the Word, and the Word was with God, and the Word was God . . . And the Word became flesh and dwelt among us, and we beheld his glory . . . " (John 1:1, 2 and 14). Many years later the apostle wrote his inspired message and as he did, probably paused and whispered: "We surely did. We saw His glory . . . the glory of the only begotten of the Father, full of grace and truth."

It was so easy to visualize the King of Glory holding court among angelic hosts. He had brought the universe into being, made flowers to grow and birds to sing. He had formed the first rainbow, and listened as the sons of God sang together for joy. Now, the Son of God was seated at the head of the table, and His eyes were pools of compassion. "Having loved his own which were in the world, he loved them unto the end" (John 13:1). Sometimes Jesus seemed to be an enigma. The arms which embraced the universe hugged children; cheeks which shone with heavenly radiance, could also be wet with tears. Their beloved Master who had been hungry before the barren fig tree, could also take a lad's lunch and supply a banquet for thousands of people. He was predicting His death, but remained unafraid. The Lord Who controlled myriads of worlds would be slain by enemies, but it was difficult to believe and harder still to understand how He remained calm and serene. Perhaps the poet captured that mood when he wrote:

> Drop Thy still dews of quietness,
> Till all our strivings cease:
> Take from our lives the strain and stress,
> And let our ordered lives confess
> The Beauty of Thy peace.

The Superb Message . . . *Sufficient*
A Different Covenant

Whether or not Peter and his colleagues understood the significance of that final Passover is questionable. It was so life-changing, that its importance may have defied immediate comprehension. When they considered the ancient feast and remembered the deliverance from Egypt, the disciples said: "God did that for them." Ever afterward when they partook of the Lord's Supper and remembered Calvary, they exclaimed: "He did that for us." The Gospel embraced all nations yet remained intensely individualistic. The blood of Christ had been shed for the remission of their sin, and through its efficacy, they had entered into a new covenant with God.

A Definite Custom

The Passover celebration was observed by Hebrews once a year, but to accommodate travelers unable to attend the first, another was held later in the year. Attendance was the responsibility of every Hebrew. It was significant that no Christian ever kept the Passover; when a believer was received into the fellowship of the church, the annual observance became unimportant. Paul went to Jerusalem to be present at the festivities only to take advantage of the opportunity of preaching to the assembled crowds. When the Savior instituted the Last Supper, He did not enclose it with rules and regulations, but simply said: "As often as ye do this, do it in remembrance of me."

A Delightful Concern

> "And he took the cup, and gave thanks, and said: Take this, and drink it among yourselves, For I say unto you, I will not drink of the fruit of the vine until the kingdom of God shall come" (Luke 22:17–18).

When the Lord looked at His followers, His soul must have been filled with compassion for they were about to become as sheep without a shepherd. When He said: "Take this and divide it among yourselves," He appeared to be urging them to encourage each other to honor His commandments. It became significant that the early church developed the custom of breaking bread every Sunday—the first day of the week. Luke wrote: "And upon the first day of the week (the first days of the weeks), when the disciples came together to break bread, Paul preached unto them . . . ." (see Acts 20:7). They came— not to hear Paul preach, but to remember their Lord. It was an additional delight to hear God's servant, but the Christians would have been there. The Passover ceremonial was no longer observed; the Holy Communion, as it came to be called, was far more important for the slain Lamb of God was risen and among His people.

At first the early Christians transformed each meal into a love feast; today believers hold such services once in a week, a month, or even a year. Some denominations favor their own method, but none are justified in condemning others who do not share their opinion. It is remarkable that after nearly two thousand years, people all over the world enjoy this special service of remembrance. Within the Central Highlands of New Guinea, the native believers use banana leaves for plates, sweet potato for bread, and colored water for wine, but the blessing of the Lord is just as real and wonderful as in the most beautiful of Europe's cathedrals. The Lord Jesus seemed to say: "I shall soon be leaving you: do not forget Me." It would be impossible for dedicated Christians to forget the Lord, for without Him life would be meaningless.

16

PETER REFUSES TO HAVE HIS FEET WASHED

"Then cometh Jesus to Simon Peter; and Peter saith unto him, Lord, dost thou wash my feet? Jesus answered and said unto him, What I do thou knowest not now; but thou shalt know hereafter. Peter saith unto him, Thou shalt never wash my feet. Jesus answered him, If I wash thee not, thou hast no part with me. Simon Peter saith unto him, Lord, not my feet only, but also my hands and my head" (John 13:6–9).

I have always wished that one of the disciples of Jesus had possessed a tape recorder. It is difficult to explain this Scripture for there are two interpretations, either of which may be correct. Was Simon Peter critical and stubborn, or sincere and subdued? Was his voice raised in strenuous argument, or quiet and restrained? When he said to the Lord: "Thou shalt never wash my feet," was he belligerent, or on the verge of shedding tears? If it were possible to listen to his voice, these questions would be answered immediately. The Lord had risen from the supper table, and pouring water into a bowl, had commenced washing the feet of His disciples. The men were surprised but silent as He proceeded, and only Peter appeared to dislike what was happening. When the Lord reached him, the disciple asked: "Lord, dost thou wash my feet?" Jesus replied: "What I do, thou knowest not now, but thou shalt know hereafter." This was to be one of the greatest lessons taught by the Lord; it would provide a foundation upon which all preaching would rest. "Yes, Peter," Jesus seemed to say, "this may seem strange, but eventually you will understand what I am doing. Your foot, please."

Peter's eyes filled with indignation as he replied: "No, Thou shalt never wash my feet." The disciples were shocked; their brother had gone too far! The Lord seemed to be considering the matter as, calmly, He sat back upon His heels. He replied: "All right, Peter, but you must understand one thing. If I do not wash you, we have nothing in common. As long as you remain with me, I must wash you. Decide what you wish to do." Poor Peter; he resembled a deflated balloon as his ego subsided.

Evidently he had to respond, for the Master awaited a reply. He almost shouted, "Not my feet only, but also my hands and my head." Even as he spoke he was thrusting his foot into the hands of the Lord. Jesus was very deliberate as He continued the washing of Peter's feet, but His head had been lowered to prevent His friend seeing the sparkle which shone in His eyes. He had planted seeds which would germinate and yield an astonishing harvest. When the foot washing was completed, Jesus again said: "You still do not understand, but soon you will know exactly what I have done. When the Spirit of Truth is come, He will explain what you need to know.

A Confusing Reaction . . . *Puzzling*

When Simon Peter objected to the washing of his feet, was he expressing pride, or humility? For example, did he say: "Lord, there is no need to wash my feet; they are clean. When I entered this room I attended to the matter, and my feet are not dirty. You may wash the other men's feet, but mine do not need cleansing." On the other hand, did he whisper: "Master, You cannot wash my feet; I am not worthy that this should be done. Let me wash Your feet."

Both ideas are still expressed. I once asked a man if he were a sinner and, utterly amazed, he replied: "Good Lord, no. I am not a sinner, I am a churchman." On the other hand, I remember an evangelistic service in the Shetland Islands when a fisherman came to the counseling room to say: "I feel black!" The Bible calls this conviction; it is the experience known by all who meet the Savior. Peter might have been proud or humble, but the end results would have been identical—he needed to be cleansed by Christ. That fact is true today as it was when Peter complained. Man can and must cleanse his body, but he remains incapable of removing sin from his soul. When Adam became a sinner, his nature became tainted, and unfortunately, this was transmitted from generation to generation. David said: "Behold, I was shapen in iniquity; and in sin did my mother conceive me" (see Psalm 51:5). Man needs a new nature which can only be given by the Savior. Jesus said to one of the most respected clergymen of His generation: "Verily, verily I say unto thee, except a man be born again, he cannot see the kingdom of God" (see John 3:3).

Nicodemus was not only a rabbi, he was a member of the Sanhedrin and morally unimpeachable and above reproach. He was a student of the Scriptures and admired by his colleagues. Nevertheless, the Savior said to him: "Marvel not that I say unto thee, Ye must be born again." That distinguished gentleman entered into the kingdom of God—not because of his eminence, but because of his acceptance of Christ. He had been trained by Hebrew professors and honored by fellow men, but only Jesus could supply what he needed. The Master was trying to teach that same lesson by supplying an object lesson of incalculable worth. Possibly Peter did not understand and was confused, but what transpired on the day of Pentecost proved he learned his lesson.

A Challenging Response . . . *Potent*

When the Lord suggested that Simon Peter could be removed from the fellowship, the man's ego was shattered. He had responded to the call of Christ, forsaken family and occupation, and acceptably preached throughout the country. When it appeared that all this might be lost, the possibilities seemed to be catastrophic. The Lord was trying to enlighten His servant regarding one of the most important facts of life. If salvation depended upon sacrifice and service, even Judas might have been saved. The betrayer had done precisely what the others had done. Jesus was emphasizing the importance of obedience; love meant more than stereotyped service. The Lord was hoping to avoid arguments which could arise each time He suggested something the disciples neither understood nor appreciated. Many of the earliest converts to Christianity would be orthodox Jews, who would need to learn the necessity of crowning Christ the Lord of their lives. Misguided men asserted there were many ways by which to reach heaven. The Master claimed this was untrue. He said: "I am the way, the truth, and the life. no man cometh unto the Father but by me" (John 14:6). Since that revelation was supplied by Christ, it remains evident that without the Savior it is impossible to become a child of God. That was to be the theme enunciated on the day of Pentecost. To repeat what has been said, whether Simon were haughty and proud or sincere and penitent, the end result would have been the same. Only the Savior could do for people what needed to be done. The final choice must be made by people; the last destiny will be decided by God.

A Complete Revelation ... *Phenomenal*

What happened on the day of Pentecost can only be described as a miracle. Neither the eloquence of a gifted orator, nor the organizing ability of a special committee could explain how an ordinary fisherman could influence thousands of people—many of whom were highly educated and extremely critical. When Simon Peter joined with others in a prayer meeting destined to last ten days, he was just an ordinary man. After that time of intercession, he emerged an irrefutable, dynamic exponent of eternal truth. Had he preached the same sermon at any time earlier in his ministry, in all probability it would have had little effect upon his listeners. It remains significant that a few days later Stephen, who was a better student and preacher than Peter, became the first Christian martyr. The people refused to accept his message, and had pleasure stoning their victim. It seems strange that the phenomenal success of Simon Peter was sandwiched between Christ's crucifixion, and the death of the first martyr of the early church.

The miracle of Pentecost was the result of the arrival of the Holy Spirit to take advantage of a special set of circumstances. An international congregation of Jews had assembled who spoke Hebrew. Had the apostles spoken in that language, they would not have paid much attention. When God's servants spoke, and in some strange manner people of many tongues understood perfectly what was being said, they were compelled to listen. That probably was the greatest miracle performed on the day of Pentecost. It should be remembered that although the multitude may have heard of the disciples, they had not met them. Yet, when Peter addressed the huge audience, although he was not a public orator, he succeeded in fascinating thousands of listeners. Words fell from his lips as a torrent of inspired information, and every man knew this was not an accident. If some of those early converts had been present when Simon Peter was scared by a servant girl and later denied his Master, they must have wondered how a coward could so quickly become a fearless speaker. When Peter explained how he had met the resurrected Christ, it became evident his testimony was worth hearing. He was not afraid of death, for his Master was alive and in charge of everything; he believed the death of Jesus had fulfilled ancient prophecies, and the Cross had become the gateway to Heaven. There was no need to fear the future, for it rested in the hand of God.

Peter and his colleagues knew that without the aid of the Holy

Spirit, they would be helpless; in union with the risen Lord the gates of Hell could not prevail against them. Within a few weeks the visitors would be returning to their homes, and each one would be an evangelist. If the Pentecostal outpouring had taken place two or three weeks later, the opportunity would have been lost. Peter's mind was enlightened in time for his message to be preached to thousands of people. God was perfectly capable of formulating His time table, and running His program on time.

17

PETER MAKES A SUGGESTION TO JOHN

"Jesus said . . . Verily, verily, I say unto you, that one of you shall betray me. Then the disciples looked one on another, doubting of whom he spake. Now there was leaning on Jesus' bosom one of the disciples, whom Jesus loved. Simon Peter therefore beckoned to him, that he should ask who it should be of whom he spake" (John 13:21–24).

When Jesus said to His disciples: "One of you shall betray me," He was deliberate and sad. He was seated at the table looking at His friends; perhaps tears were in His eyes. His followers were bewildered, for it seemed inconceivable that one of their number could be capable of such a dastardly deed. Surely their Master was taking things a little too far! Honorable men could not do what had been suggested. The incident might have passed, but as usual Peter could not be silent. He was hesitant to speak, for only a few minutes earlier he had argued with the Lord about the necessity of feet washing, and had no wish to be involved in another altercation. Nevertheless, he believed that if a traitor were within the fellowship, the man should be exposed. Simon desired to know the identity of the betrayer but did not ask the Lord, for maybe he feared to hear his own name. Most men would have remained silent, but this apostle had an explosive soul and could not quell its uprisal. John was close to the Lord, and Peter gestured to him to ask the name of the guilty brother.

"He then lying on Jesus' breast saith unto him, Lord, who is it? Jesus answered, He it is, to whom I shall give a sop, when I have dipped it. And when he had dipped the sop, he gave it to Judas Iscariot, the son of Simon. And after the sop Satan entered into him. Then said Jesus unto him, That thou doest, do quickly. Now no man at the table knew for what intent he spake this unto him. For some of them thought, that because

Judas had the bag, that Jesus had said unto him, Buy those things that we have need of against the feast; or that he should give something to the poor. He then having received the sop went immediately out: and it was night" (John 13:25–30).

The Unknown Betrayer . . . *Love Unfathomable*

When the Lord announced that one of the disciples would become a traitor, it seemed the sun had been eclipsed. It was beyond credibility that one of their fellowship could be so depraved. It was even more difficult to understand how the other members of the party could be unaware of the betrayer's identity. Jesus and Judas had been together for three years, and the only official position within the party, that of treasurer, had been given to him. It is not known how money became available, but probably grateful people donated love offerings which were controlled by Judas. The men had been together for a long time, and the other disciples had many opportunities to observe the conduct of each other. It was almost impossible for the Lord to live with Judas without revealing disapproval.

Had any other men been in the same situation, they would have indicated that Judas was not the man he was supposed to be. It is extremely thought-provoking that when Jesus announced the presence of a betrayer, the other disciples had no idea whom that would be. They would be expected to say: "That must be Judas. We have seen this coming for a long time." It was amazing that even John was taken by surprise. Simon Peter was the man who generally knew more about his colleagues than they knew about themselves. He was the inquisitive disciple who had difficulty curbing his curiosity. Yet even he was startled by the Lord's announcement. Quickly he looked at John who was reclining against the Master, and motioning with his hands, suggested the Lord be asked to name the offender. It seemed unbelievable that any of the men would commit such a crime, but evidently Jesus believed otherwise. That unreliable man should be exposed, and Peter wanted John to do something about the matter. The Savior readily complied with the request, but His reply only deepened the mystery.

It is important to know that when a host wished to show favor toward a special guest, he gave to him a special portion which was called "a sop." This act was recognized to be a commendation, an offer of friendship. The last act of the Lord toward Judas was therefore very meaningful. Unfortunately, this was rejected. It was easy for the Devil to enter into Judas, for the door had been left open! When the Lord said: "That thou doest, do quickly," the listening disciples still did not understand what was meant. They thought Judas was being commissioned to purchase urgently needed supplies, or that assistance should be given to poor people. They realized that someone might be false, but even in their wildest imagination could not believe Judas would be he.

Some people find difficulty in understanding why Judas was invited to become one of the followers of Christ. He was called "The Son of Perdition"—the son of Satan, and as such was thrust upon the Lord. Had Jesus refused the challenge, evil hosts would have accused Him of cowardice. Could He maintain His purity when a snake lay in His bosom? Eventually, Satan took complete control of the deluded man, but prior to that moment, Judas made his own decisions. He was not compelled to betray the Lord, for he was surrounded by the love of God. Regrettably, even the overtures of Divine Compassion failed to turn him from his evil intentions. When he persisted in his evil behavior, even Peter and John failed to recognize what was taking place. If the traitor had been virtuous, he might have been able to sing:

> Oh, the deep, deep love of Jesus
> Vast, unmeasured, boundless, free:
> Rolling as a mighty ocean,
> In its fullness over me.

The Unusual Beckoning . . . *Love Uninformed*

It was evident that Jesus knew from the beginning the identity of His enemy, but He preserved His secret. The Savior shared many things with John, but this information was never divulged to anyone. If in some unfortunate manner it had become known, all fellowship among the followers of the Lord would have been ruined. It is always wise to speak of good deeds, but evil actions are better forgotten. If all Christians observed this rule, the church and the world would be enriched.

The Pharisees were proud of their self-righteousness, but were unconcerned when making other people sin. As long as they did not stain their own garments of conceit, they cared not what happened to other people. Jesus accused them of being whited sepulchres—clean on the outside, and filthy within. When Paul wrote to the Ephesians he said: "Let no corrupt communication proceed out of your mouth, but that which is good . . . all bitterness and . . . evil speaking be put away from you . . ." (Ephesians 4:29, 31). The apostle detested distasteful conversations, for he knew gossip poisoned the soul and destroyed fellowship. The Scriptures emphasize the importance of being Christlike, but they also warn against becoming stumbling blocks to other people. When Christ refrained from identifying the betrayer, He protected His friends, and provided an example for everybody.

The Urgent Bidding . . . *Love Unrestricted*

"That thou doest, do quickly" (John 13:27).

It is distressing to note that after Satan entered into Judas Iscariot, the Lord said: "That thou doest, do quickly." He urged the wicked man not to linger, for that would only increase his misery and condemnation. Judas had reached the place where nothing could save his soul. The Lord's offer of friendship had been rejected, and the guilty man in his own perverted way had decided "God helps those who help themselves." Already he was calculating how much money could be made by assisting the Pharisees. He thought he was leaving a ship before it sank, or thatching his house before the arrival of a storm. Jesus must have been exceedingly sorrowful as He watched the destruction of a man He loved. He could not prevent the tragedy.

One wonders what Simon Peter thought as he watched the unfolding of the calamity. Did he become enraged and desire to take the law into his own hands? Eventually he was so overwhelmed with his own shame, that it was impossible to blame anyone but himself. His own unfaithfulness forbade the condemnation of others. Judas, who had been so near to the kingdom of God, had failed to enter. Did that realization kindle a fire within the heart of the man destined to win thousands of souls on the day of Pentecost? Did the fall of Judas help to raise Peter to unprecedented heights of success?

Peter knew it was possible to be within a step of God's kingdom and yet miss it by a mile! When endued by the Spirit of God, he confronted the crowds in Jerusalem—that wisdom enriched his testimony. The apostle remembered how the Master had said: "If I wash thee not, thou hast no part with me." That object lesson was clearly in his mind when he said: "Neither is there salvation in any other, for there is none other name under heaven given among men whereby we must be saved" (see Acts 4:12). Simon Peter had learned his lesson.

18

PETER RUNS A STOPLIGHT
AND GETS INTO TROUBLE

"And the Lord said, Simon, Simon, behold, Satan hath desired to have you, that he may sift you as wheat. But I have prayed for thee that thy faith fail not, and when thou art converted [turned back again], strengthen thy brethren. And he said unto him, Lord, I am ready to go with thee, both into prison and to death" (Luke 22:31–33).

Warnings are not objects of amusement; they are meant to prevent accidents. When a road becomes unsafe for travel, special signs are erected to inform people of approaching areas of danger. Intelligent travelers observe those signs. If buildings are unsafe, inhabitants are evacuated to other areas; when fire threatens to destroy districts, residents are requested to leave. The same facts relate to human bodies. Certain pains are considered to be warnings of worse things to follow, and sufferers are advised to consult a doctor in the hope of preventing serious illness. Within the modern world citizens are accustomed to traffic signals installed by civic authorities; to ignore them is a punishable offense. Red traffic lights mean one thing—STOP! Unfortunately, for one reason or another, people violate these laws, but offenders invite disaster. Simon Peter was guilty of such an offense. He was very foolish when he ignored a special warning issued by the Savior. If modern terms can be used, he ran through a red light!

People who talk a lot often betray their insecurity. They say they can do everything, but fear responsibility. Peter provided evidence to support that assertion. He sounded as though he could remove mountains, but a speck of dirt in his eye could ruin his vision. He was annoyed when the Lord said: "Simon, Simon, Satan hath desired to have you that he may sift you as wheat." Actually he should have been elated, for the Devil is seldom disturbed by inactive Christians.

Simon was a little arrogant. He was convinced of his own capabilities and said in so many words: "Master, You need not worry about me. I am more than a match for the Devil or anyone else. I am ready to go with Thee, both into prison and to death. If the Devil comes after me, I will do with him as David did with Goliath—I will demolish him."

The Terrible Testing . . . *Devastating*

He should have considered the scriptures. To assist people in need, God arranged cities of refuge, the gates of which never closed. A man could enter at any time of the day or night. Yet the stipulation imposed by the law stated that the person concerned was protected only inside the refuge. If he remained outside of the national shelter, the Avenger of Blood was permitted to attack him. During the lifetime of the Lord many people recognized He was the fulfillment of the ancient type. He said: "Come unto me, all ye that labour and are heavy laden, and I will give you rest" (Matthew 11:28). When men refuse to accept that invitation, they ask for trouble. People are safe only when they are in Christ!

Many years later when Peter had been enriched by his own experiences, he wrote to his friends saying: "Be sober, be vigilant; because your adversary the devil, as a roaring lion, walketh about, seeking whom he may devour" (1 Peter 5:8). If he, earlier in life, had accepted the same advice offered by the Lord, tragedy would have been avoided. Confidence may be an asset, but when accompanied by humility and trust, it is infinitely better. Christians should remember that the enemy of souls is not only aware of our weaknesses; he knows how to exploit them. As long as an antelope sees a lion it is moderately safe, but the larger beast hides in the bushes until a false sense of security destroys the victim. Men aware of their need flee to the Savior, but if they remain inactive and indifferent they are always in peril.

When the Lord warned Simon Peter, the red lights of warning began to glow in the disciple's mind, but unfortunately the fisherman's wisdom was overshadowed by arrogance. Within hours his voice which had proudly announced: "Thou art the Christ, the Son of the living God," was denying all knowledge of his best Friend.

The Thrilling Testimony . . . *Disclosure*

"But I have prayed for thee that thy faith fail not, and when thou art converted, strengthen thy brethren" (Luke 22:32).

The Savior looked beyond Peter at his worst to see him at his best. Instead of criticizing the disgraced disciple, Jesus prayed for him, and that intercession turned a tragedy into a triumph. Simon resembled the man who went down from Jerusalem to Jericho and fell among thieves, who stripped him of his raiment and wounded him leaving him half dead. Describing that man's misfortune the late Dr. Parker of London used to say: "He asked for it! Any man who turns his back on the altar of God to go down to the city of the curse, deserves to fall among thieves. He asked for it!"

When dealing with such characters, most men emulate the example set by the priest and the Levite; they remain indifferent. But "the good Samaritan went to him and bound up his wounds, pouring in oil and wine, and set him on his own beast, and brought him to an inn, and took care of him" (see Luke 10:33–34). The Lord's prayer for Peter was invaluable; the man could not perish when the long arm of Christ's love held him. Dr. S. D. Gordon of Boston said: "The love of Christ is like a cord; one end is fastened in the heart of God, the other in the heart of man. That cord *is like elastic, it will stretch but not break.* When a man wanders from God the love-cord stretches and stretches, and the more it does, the greater becomes the tug on both ends. There is a pull in God's heart because He has lost a child; there is another in man's soul because he has lost a Father. There is reason to believe that when Peter fell, the tragedy hurt the Master as much as it did the man." The disappointing fisherman was experiencing something later expressed by George Matheson:

> O Love that wilt not let me go
> I rest my weary soul on Thee:
> I give Thee back the life I owe
> That in Thine ocean depths its flow
> May richer, fuller be.

The Tremendous Triumph . . . *Delighting*

The question has been asked: What would have happened to Simon Peter had not the Lord prayed for him? The answer is swiftly forthcoming. The same that would happen to us if Christ did not pray for us. The writer to the Hebrews said: "Wherefore Christ is able to save them to the uttermost that come unto God by him, *seeing he ever liveth to make intercession for them*" (see Hebrews 7:25).

His Concern

Peter's disgrace would soon be overwhelming; he would probably wish to die. The Lord might have remained silent, but He cared for His servant and was trying to soften the blow about to fall. He was attempting to say that whatever happened, nothing could separate Peter from "the love of God, which was in Christ Jesus" (see Romans 8:38–39).

His Confidence

The Lord wanted Peter to remember the loss of a battle did not mean the end of a war. Setbacks would come, but even failures could be transformed into stepping stones by which a fallen man could regain his feet. Jesus knew Peter would rise again to face the challenges of the future, and spoke about his restoration. He said: "When thou art converted, strengthen thy brethren."

His Consideration

How could he correct, advise or edify his brethren? They would be aware of his hypocritical behavior, and would pay no attention to anything he said. His ministry had terminated! The Lord knew otherwise—the future was destined to be glorious. He seemed to be saying: "Peter, do not permit shame to silence your voice. I want you to strengthen your brethren, for they like you will need all the encouragement obtainable. Permitting Satan to hush your testimony will only compound the problem. I have prayed for you that thy faith fail not. I am depending upon you to complete what you commenced. Do not disappoint Me."

HOMILY NO. 5

Christ's Prayer for Peter

The atmosphere in the upper room was tense. Incredulity had given place to indignation, and Peter's eyes were expressing the rising feelings of his heart. The other disciples were listening, and Peter resented this statement of his Lord. It was preposterous that He should suggest such a thing. Had He no confidence in His followers? Peter's eyes swept around the little gathering. Almost imperceptibly his chin was pushed out, and his hands became fists. "Lord, what are you saying?" "And the Lord said, Simon, Simon, behold, Satan hath desired to have you, that he may sift you as wheat: But I have prayed for thee, that thy faith fail not: and when thou art converted, strengthen thy brethren." Peter's eyes became pin-points of anger; his lips pursed, then, "Lord, I am ready to go with thee, both into prison, and to death." His statement was an outburst and a challenge. The other disciples might be unreliable, but he would never disown his Lord! And Jesus quietly answered, "Peter, the cock shall not crow this day, before that thou shalt thrice deny that thou knowest me . . . *But I have prayed for thee.*"

The Vision of His Prayer

The Lord Jesus was never taken by surprise, and consequently was never rash in words nor actions. Every major decision in His ministry was preceded by a period of communion, when God gave the guidance so necessary to Christ's inspired ministry. Probably, during one of these times of prayer, the conviction deepened that all was not well with Simon. It became so clear to the Lord. Peter would slip into the shadows; his hold upon eternal realities would weaken; his future would be in jeopardy! Then the Lord's face revealed the holy determination in His heart. His lips moved and He prayed, and that unrecorded prayer proved to be Peter's lifeline when the coming storm swirled around his soul.

The Virtue of His Prayer

It is noteworthy that the Lord never mentioned the matter to his self-confident disciple until the secret battle had been fought and won. Perhaps other people acquainted with such knowledge would have uttered loud and persistent condemnation of the unreliable Simon. Within seconds a fiery argument could have filled the little sanctuary with strife. So often one hasty word has been a match to start a devastating fire, and before the conflagration has been extinguished, blackened scars have appeared on the souls of men and women. This never happened with the Lord Jesus for His times of prayer were constant safeguards against the activities of evil. He won the battle for Peter's soul even before the disciple heard there would be a battle.

The Value of His Prayer

"When thou art converted, strengthen thy brethren." The Lord not only saw the approaching tragedy, He looked beyond to see the new Peter resplendent in the power of a new life. Christ was certain that

His prayer would be answered. He had wrestled in the secret place and the issue was no longer in doubt. Possibly He had no wish to prevent the coming of the time of testing. He preferred that Simon should undergo the trial, for afterward the disciple would emerge a better and a stronger man. We are persuaded that since the ultimate triumph was won in prayer, it was not possible for Simon to be lost. Each time the waves of remorse and guilt threatened to sweep the despairing man to oblivion, the strong arms of redeeming love brought him closer to safety.

The Victory of His Prayer

"It was all over. A sickening silence had fallen upon the people around the fire; their questionings had ceased. Yet within the mind of a haunted man, a deafening clamor had broken loose. The searing sword of conscience was playing havoc with his peace of mind. Sweeping aside the onlookers, Peter ran into the night—he had failed; he had disowned his Lord, he was a disgrace! And within the courthouse the Lord was calm. There was no need to worry, for already poor tormented Peter was safe in the arms of a Father's kindness. Later, when the Lord looked down from heaven to see a new man telling forth the word of life on the day of Pentecost, surely His great heart throbbed with thanksgiving; He was so glad He had prayed for Peter. The denial had become a stepping stone to unprecedented triumphs. And because the Lord loves to do things of this nature, He prays for all His followers. There are times when He says, 'Father, remember Ivor Powell. Things are becoming difficult and dangerous in his experience.' Reader, there are times when He prays for YOU. I'm thrilled—are you?" (Reprinted from the author's commentary, *Luke's Thrilling Gospel*, Kregel Publications, Grand Rapids, Michigan.)

19

PETER BECOMES A TOUR GUIDE

". . . and his disciples came to him to shew him the buildings of the temple" (Matthew 24:1).

"And Jesus answering said, Seest thou these great buildings? There shall not be left one stone upon another that shall not be thrown down. And as he sat upon the Mount of Olives over against the temple, Peter and James and John and Andrew asked him private-ly, Tell us, when shall these things be? and what shall be the sign when all these things shall be fulfilled? (Mark 13:2–4).

During the passing of the centuries, innumerable guides have es-corted visitors through the city of Jerusalem. The vast majority of these men and women proved themselves to be a source of informa-tion and inspiration. Some were of Arab descent; others were Jewish, but all were well informed and sensitive to the faith of visitors. It is extremely interesting to know that nearly two thousand years ago the disciples who had been admiring the massive structure of the temple, came to Jesus and enthusiastically invited Him to tour the sanctuary. Possibly they overlooked the fact that their Master had visited the place earlier, and was already acquainted with the magnificent build-ing. The Lord accepted their invitation, but seemed disturbed as He listened to the conversation of the disciples. They, in retrospect, con-sidered how the huge stone blocks had been placed in position. He was looking ahead to the time when the temple would be destroyed.

"And as he went forth out of the temple, one of his disciples saith unto him, Master, behold, what manner of stones and what manner of buildings!" This would be in the evening. According to St. Luke (xxi. 37), our Lord, during the early part of this week, passed His nights upon the Mount of Olives, taking His food at Bethany with Martha and Mary, and spending His days in the temple at Jerusalem teaching the people. It is most probable that He left the temple by the golden gate on the east from whence the view of the temple would be particularly striking. We learn from St. Matthew that our Lord had just been predicting the fall of Jerusalem. It was therefore natural for the disciples to call His attention at that moment to the grandeur and beauty of the building and its surroundings.

"The temple at Jerusalem was one of the wonders of the world. Josephus says that it had everything the eye and the mind could admire. It shone with a fiery splendor, so that when the eye gazed thereon it turned away as from the rays of the sun. The size of the foundation stones was enormous. Josephus speaks of some of the stones as forty-five cubits in length, five in height, and six in breadth. One of the foundation stones measured in recent times, proved to be nearly twenty-four feet in length by four feet in depth. But all this magnificence had no effect upon our Lord, Who only repeated the sentence of its downfall" (quoted from *The Pulpit Commentary*, Mark's Gospel, Wm. B. Eerdmans Publishing Co., Grand Rapids, Michigan).

The Lord listened as His friends discussed the size of the stones and praised the skill of the architects who devised methods of moving them. They were surprised when He suddenly said: "Seest thou these great stone buildings? There shall not be left one stone upon another that shall not be thrown down." He seemed as a prophet looking down the corridors of time to behold the terrible tragedy which a few years later destroyed the entire complex. His prediction was so terrifying that the conversation of the disciples came to an abrupt halt. Later, as they rested upon the Mount of Olives where it was possible to see the magnificent structure, four of His disciples, Peter, James, John and Andrew said: "Master you predicted the fall of the temple. When will this happen?" As was to be expected, Peter was probably the spokesman for the group. "Master, you said these blocks of stone would be removed one by one until the building would be demolished. Who will commit such sacrilege, and why? Lord, we would like to hear more." It is evident from Matthew's Gospel the disciples associated the destruction of the temple with the end of the world and the return of Christ to the earth. The Savior's initial task was the separation of these events so that His followers would not be misinformed.

The Destruction of the Temple

The information given by the Savior was precise and detailed. The world now knows that Christ's prediction was literally fulfilled in the year A.D. 70 when the Roman general, Titus, overran the city. The account given by Josephus was very graphic. The destruction of the Holy City remains one of the world's greatest tragedies. Rivers of blood flowed through the gates when vast numbers of Jews were slaughtered by ruthless enemies. The ancient writer added a footnote to his manuscript in which he said that as far as one could only see, were crucified Jews who had suffered that fate because they had similarly killed their Messiah.

Describing the end of the siege, Josephus told how a courageous band of young Hebrews shut themselves in the temple and fought as long as they were able. Then as a final act of defiance, they set alight the sanctuary and died in the conflagration which followed. The Romans who wanted the gold were compelled to wait several days before they could approach the temple; the stones were so hot they could not be touched. When days had passed the men carefully dismantled the walls, taking them down stone by stone, hoping to discover the precious metal which had melted and penetrated into cracks in the walls. Thus were the words of the Savior literally fulfilled. "There shall not be left one stone upon another that shall not be thrown down."

The only surviving part of that temple has become a shrine in Israel. What was formerly known as The Wailing Wall is now called The Great West Wall. An Israeli politician recently said: "Some day we may be able to dig in this area, and who can tell what might be discovered! That wall will become part of the new temple which will be erected on this site." Time will tell whether or not his statement will be accurate.

The Dissemination of the Truth

"And this gospel of the kingdom shall be preached in all the world for a witness unto all nations; AND THEN SHALL THE END COME" (Matthew 24:14).

It is evident from the teaching of the New Testament that the early Christians expected the Lord to return to earth during their lifetime. They had either misinterpreted or forgotten the words of the Savior. It should be remembered that for many of those people the world was not as large as it is now known to be; it was only the size of the Roman Empire. The citizens of the first century had no knowledge of the undiscovered world, and when Paul had completed his missionary journeys many believed all nations had been evangelized. Until recent times millions of people had never heard the Gospel. Then missionary enterprise began to spread the message around the world, and today modern technology has revolutionized communications. Radio and television have accomplished things thought to be unachievable. Today it would be difficult to find nations where the opportunity to listen to the Gospel is not possible. It is thought-provoking that countries which formerly were unevangelized, are sending preachers to America and Europe.

The Lord said: "And the gospel of the kingdom shall be preached in all the world for a testimony unto them and *THEN* shall the end come." It has been claimed that this applies solely to the time when Hebrew young men will visit all nations to tell of the Savior's reign in Jerusalem, but be that as it may, the spread of the message over such vast areas can only be done with the aid of modern technology. This fact is sufficient to endorse the claim that the return of Christ to earth will soon become a reality.

It was significant that when the Lord predicted the spread of the Gospel, He also stated there would be an outbreak of heresy. He said the lies of Satan would be so convincing that even the elect would be threatened. John became aware of this danger and warned readers against false teachers (see 1 John 4:1–3). Paul was so convinced of the authenticity of his message, that he pronounced a curse on all preachers who contradicted his doctrines (see Galatians 1:8). The incarnation of the Son of God; redemption through the blood shed at Calvary; His resurrection and ascension to become the High Priest of His people were the basic principles of God's Gospel. Denial of these facts was considered blasphemous.

There have always been earthquakes, pestilences and wars among nations, but there has never been as many sects and cults as there are today. The world unfortunately tolerates movements which our founding fathers would have forbidden. Under the cloak of free speech men can say anything they desire. The Lord predicted that in the end times many professed believers would become cold and indifferent, and some would become prominent in false religious movements. He also said that when such things became visible, then would the end come. The spread of false teaching would precede His return to earth. It can hardly be called a coincidence that the signs He mentioned can now be seen.

Jesus stated that in the closing days of this age, the Abomination of Desolation would stand in the Holy Place to denounce the living God. That designated place may be within the Jewish temple, or it could be in Jerusalem which has always been called "The Holy City." When the Lord spoke about conditions to come, He predicted that unprecedented problems would afflict the inhabitants of earth; the Great Tribulation would surpass anything known to man. The nations of earth have always suffered from international conflicts, but modern leaders are becoming increasingly worried about the future. This is exactly what Jesus predicted when He sat that day upon the Mount of Olives.

The Definite Triumph

"And in those days, after that tribulation, the sun shall be darkened, and the moon shall not give her light. And the stars of heaven shall fall, and the powers that are in heaven shall be shaken. And then shall they see the Son of man coming in the clouds with great power and glory" (Mark 13:24–26).

After his denial of the Lord, Simon Peter "remembered the word of the Lord" (Luke 22:61). It is now evident that statement applies to other incidents in his life. When John Mark left Paul and Barnabas to return to Jerusalem he was in disgrace, for he had deserted two of the finest Christians of his generation. The lad's future might have been in jeopardy but for the kindness of Peter who, so to speak, took the young man under his wing. Mark became the apostle's companion and secretary, and from the copious notes made during Peter's sermons, the second Gospel was produced. It is therefore evident that the words concerning the end times were remembered by the apostle, and transcribed by his young protégé. Peter had not forgotten the day when, with the other disciples, he had done the work of a tour guide. It was at that time he sat enthralled as he listened to Jesus speaking of things to come.

It is easy to imagine the two men speaking of those memorable moments. Were the eyes of Mark shining with amazement as he said: "Brother Peter, did the Lord really say these huge stones would be removed one by one? But who would take the trouble to do that; these blocks are huge and heavy." "Yes, my boy, Jesus predicted that and many other things. For example, He said the people on earth would see His descent from the skies to establish His kingdom. He will keep that promise, for His triumph is inevitable. But son, until that happens, we have a job to do. The Lord said that first the Gospel must be preached to all the nations, and that is our responsibility."

> We've a story to tell to the nations,
>   That shall turn their hearts to the right.
> A story of truth and mercy
>   A story of peace and light.
>
> For the darkness shall turn to dawning
>   And the dawning to noon-day bright;
> And Christ's great kingdom shall come on earth
>   The kingdom of love and light.

—Colin Stern (1862–1928)

20

PETER WOUNDS AN ENEMY

"Then Simon Peter having a sword drew it, and smote the high priest's servant, and cut off his right ear. The servant's name was Malchus. Then said Jesus unto Peter, Put up thy sword into the sheath. The cup which my Father hath given me, shall I not drink it?" (John 18:10–11).

The Garden of Gethsemane was hushed; no sound could be heard except for the whisper of the wind in the trees, or the cry of a night bird returning to its nest. It was the stillness preceding a storm, for on the opposite hill the gates of Jerusalem were opening to permit the exit of a murderous crowd. Led by Judas and the detestable Pharisees, six hundred soldiers were to arrest the troublesome Nazarene and bring Him to justice. Their lanterns were like giant fireflies dancing in the night. Jesus remained calm, but His friends were apprehensive. Most of the disciples were fearful, but Simon Peter prepared to fight. If this problem led to his decease, at least he would have company as he entered into eternity. He had never been a coward, and if the enemies were to attack Jesus, their efforts would meet resistance.

Things were confusing for the determined disciple, for he had seen how one statement from the Master had demolished the opposition. Perhaps he thought the Master was too kind to hurt anyone, and decided to take matters into his own hands.

The Greek word translated *band* is *speiran* and according to Dr. J. H. Thayer, it signifies the tenth of a legion—six hundred men. This was a military operation and not a casual arrest by officers of the law. Answering a question the Lord said: *"I AM*, and when He had said this, they went backward and fell to the ground" (John 18:6). The true nature of the Son of God had momentarily broken through the frail barrier of flesh, and the result was astounding. The soldiers collapsed at His feet. Christ held them in the palm of His hand and could have crushed them; instead He permitted the regaining of their feet, and that was too much for the agitated disciple who had struck an enemy. His courage was commendable, but his wisdom nonexistent.

"Peter can hardly be blamed for his inability to recognize the hand of God working amid the unpleasant events of that night. His impetuosity in acting without the expressed permission of his Leader may be understood, but not condoned. A good soldier is a man under authority; rash action on the part of an unauthorized individual can lose a campaign. Probably Peter struck with the determination to slay the first man to lay hands on the Master. Mercifully, he misjudged his aim, for the servant lost his ear and not his head. 'We may add that the *life* of Malchus was safe while Christ was there, for none ever died in His presence' (A. W. Pink). When Christ returned good for evil, when the servant was healed by the power of the One he had come to take, the man was provided with memories which in after days haunted him. If he ever told his story in the high priest's palace, we may be sure the Holy Spirit used the testimony to convict every hearer. The Lord had said, 'Ye have heard that it hath been said, Thou shalt love thy neighbor, and hate thine enemy. But I say unto you love your enemies, bless them that curse you, do good to them that hate you, and pray for them which despitefully use you, and persecute you' (Matthew 5:43–44). The words written in Luke 22:50–51 supply overwhelming evidence that the Lord practiced what He preached. John omits the details to be found in the synoptic gospels; he was more concerned with the predominant fact that what was taking place, had been planned in the eternal counsels of heaven.

"The statement, 'The cup which my Father hath given me,' seems to be most thought-provoking. A cup suggests limitations. The experience through which the Son was about to pass would indeed be grievous but it would end; the cup would soon be empty. Christ saw not the bitterness of the cross; He saw and recognized the Father's will. The sweetness of being in true accord with God provided the antidote to the agony of any suffering to be endured. This was the way the Father had planned; any other would have been unthinkable" (quoted from the author's commentary, *John's Wonderful Gospel*, pp. 372–73, Kregel Publications, Grand Rapids, Michigan).

Was the life of Malchus saved by Peter's poor aim, or by a sudden push from the Almighty? If the blow had been an inch or two to the right the servant would have died immediately. It was amazing when Jesus retrieved the severed member; gently brushing away any grass,

He miraculously restored it from whence it came. What followed was even more fascinating.

> "Then said Jesus unto him, Thinkest thou that I cannot now pray to my Father and he shall presently give me more than twelve legions of angels? But how then shall the scriptures be fulfilled that thus it must be?" (Matthew 26:52–53).

When Jesus said in response to Peter's action, "Thinkest thou that I cannot now pray to my Father, and he shall presently give me more than twelve legions of angels," He uttered truths almost beyond comprehension. A legion was made up of 6,000 soldiers. Therefore, twelve legions would represent 72,000 men. That number would have been more than sufficient to meet the challenge given by the enemies in the Garden of Gethsemane. It is the hypothetical picture behind the statement that is frightening. We are informed in 2 Kings 19:35 " . . . that the angel of the LORD went out, and smote in the camp of the Assyrians an hundred fourscore and five thousand: and . . . in the morning, behold, they were all dead corpses." If one angel could slay 185,000 men, we are left to speculate as to the efficiency of twelve legions. By the same computation they could have destroyed 11 billion, 920 million, or nearly three times the population of Earth at the time when this commentary is being written. The Lord expressed the truth enshrined in the spiritual: "He's got the whole world in His hands." This only emphasized the astounding fact that Jesus was crucified—not because He was sentenced by a judge, but rather because that was the way He chose to die!

The Lord's struggle and prayer in the Garden of Gethsemane provided one of the most intimate glimpses of the Savior's suffering. It would be illuminating to know who saw and described all that took place. Peter, James and John slept through that terrible ordeal; eight other disciples were outside the hallowed garden, and Judas was assisting the enemy. Many theologians believe the informant who described the events of that fateful night was John Mark, the young man who fled leaving his cloak in the hands of a mob of hooligans. There exists the possibility that Simon or one of the other two disciples awakened to behold the poignant scene. Maybe Peter later heard the details of what had happened and certain facts became evident.

The Superb Confidence

The Savior was completely calm when many soldiers were about to arrest Him. He knew that actually they were powerless. When the Lord spoke, the small army fell helplessly at His feet, and it was evident Jesus was in control of the situation.

The Special Compassion

Why Malchus, the servant of the high priest, was close to the Lord was never revealed. Was he a spy hoping to gain information for his master? Perhaps the fact that his right ear was severed suggests he was eavesdropping. The Lord displayed kindness to an enemy and demonstrated His heart was filled with compassion. It was the same love which motivated Jesus when He said: "Father, forgive them, for they know not what they do" (Luke 23:34).

The Serious Collapse

The disciples were probably surprised when the Lord did not resist the aggression. When He permitted the soldiers to bind and lead Him away, it was more than they could endure. "And they all forsook him, and fled" (Mark 14:50). They ran into the night; scrambled up the steep hill to hide while they regained their breath. Eventually, Peter approached an intersection to see the Lord being led into a hall. His soul was filled with turmoil. Should he run to the Lord to offer what support was possible, or think of himself and find a hiding place? This was a great problem, but he could not abandon his Master. It was during these terrible moments that the words of the Lord shone brilliantly amid human failure. "I have prayed for thee, that thy faith fail not."

> When I fear my faith will fail
>   Christ will hold me fast.
> When the tempter would prevail,
>   He can hold me fast.
>
> He will hold me fast,
>   He will hold me fast,
> For my Savior loves me so;
>   He will hold me fast.

> —Ada R. Habershon

21

PETER SAT AT A FIRE AND WAS BURNED

"And when they had kindled a fire in the midst of the hall, and were set down together, Peter sat down among them" (Luke 22:55).

Overconfidence can become a source of great danger; often when people vow never to do certain things, they do them. Naaman, the Syrian leper, said he would never wash in the river Jordan, but he did. Probably Judas said he would never betray the Lord, but unfortunately he did. Simon Peter vehemently denied that he would ever be unfaithful to his Master, but he was. These experiences should be warnings to all who have inflated egos. It is always wiser to avoid danger than to attempt to overcome it. Children are advised never to play with fire, but occasionally their parents need to learn the same lesson. Throughout summer months in California, people are asked not to light fires in the mountains, for even sparks can cause terrible tragedies. Simon Peter sat too long at an enemy's fire, and inevitably he was burned!

The First Mistake

"Then took they him [Jesus] and led him, and brought him into the high priest's house. And Peter followed afar off" (Luke 22:54).

Simon was very sincere when he insisted he would never deny the Lord, but he made a fatal mistake when he allowed too much distance to come between the Master and himself. It was true that he remained a follower, but he was no longer close to the Lord. Dodging around street corners in the middle of the night was never a comforting experience; it was not a cause for amazement when Peter became cold. The poor man probably never realized how chilled he was until he saw the enemies' fire inside the hall. The Big Fishermen, as he has been called, became the prototype of all backsliders. Unfortunately millions of people have made the same mistakes. It is a safe assumption that John never lost his love while leaning on the bosom of Christ, and neither will any other. When people drift or fall away from the church, spiritual fervor disappears and danger threatens. When Christians become too involved in material activities and cease attending the house of God, when their Bible is seldom read and fellowship with other believers is rejected, spiritual temperature falls. No man can afford to become lukewarm (see Revelation 2:3–16).

The Second Mistake

"And when she [the maid] saw Peter warming himself, she looked upon him, and said: And thou also was with Jesus of Nazareth" (Mark 14:67).

When Simon Peter reached the hall, he became attracted by the fire. He never realized how cold he had become until he felt the warmth of the flames. It may be significant that when the young woman saw him "he was warming himself." Probably he had only just joined the company, and finding an open space near the fireplace, was warming his hands. He must have been a very uneasy man, for he was as a fish out of water. If his conscience troubled him, he probably decided to warm his hands for a few moments and then leave the building. Once again he provided an example which many people followed. Believers separated from Christ always lose their fervor. It is never wise to play with danger. Company is more desirable than loneliness; warmth is better than chills, but Christians who feel at home among the Lord's enemies are capable of going anywhere and doing anything. Conscience says: "This is no place for you. Get out." To ignore that advice is to invite disaster.

The Third Mistake

"And when they had kindled a fire in the midst of the hall, and were sat down together, Peter sat down among them" (Luke 22:55).

One of the men sitting at the fire probably saw the shivering stranger, and making room for him, invited Peter to join the company. He expressed his thanks and decided that not all the people present were evil. Yet, had he been closer to God, he might have heard a sigh! He resembled a fly which had walked into a web! It would be impossible to count the people who made a similar mistake.

117

Christians cannot be at peace among people who detest the Savior. A believer who once leaned upon the bosom of the Lord cannot find happiness living without the Lord. It is impossible to stay at the enemies' fire without getting burned! Backsliders never vary; separated from the Savior they become indifferent to spiritual reality and desire company which can only be harmful.

The Fourth Mistake

Simon Peter denied Christ on three occasions, but each was different. First, he denied his Lord.

> "But a certain maid beheld him as he sat by the fire and earnestly looked upon him, and said: This man was also with HIM. And he denied HIM, saying, Woman, I know HIM not" (Luke 22:56–57).

It would be informative to know where the girl first saw Simon Peter. She said: "This man was also with Jesus of Nazareth." Possibly she had seen them together—perhaps in a service where the Lord had helped an afflicted person. On the other hand she might have been in the vicinity when Jesus was being escorted on a tour of the temple. It was significant that she said: "This man was with him." If a professing Christian were challenged in some questionable place, it is always easier to admit he attends a church than to confess his adoration of the Son of God. The first denial always concerns the Lord.

I recently heard the testimony of a famous pianist who was asked how he became a Christian. He played in a band and had wandered far from the Savior. One night in a cocktail lounge, he casually asked the bartender if he were a Christian. The man replied: "Don't tell me you are a Christian. You could never be one while you stay with this crowd. They drink, gamble, do drugs, and are evil men. Nobody could follow Jesus and stay with them." The musician went down to the beach and decided it was necessary to be all or nothing for the Lord. Peter first denied the Savior—"I know HIM not."

The Fifth Mistake

> "And after a little while another saw him and said: Thou art also of them. And Peter said, Man, I am not" (Luke 22:58).

An old saying suggests that one thing leads to another! The aim of Satan is not to hinder God's people, but to destroy them. After Peter had denied his Lord, he refused to be identified with his brethren. "I am not of them!" When backsliding people begin to turn away from the Lord, they lose their desire to attend the church, and their indifference increases until it seems like a mountain hiding the sun. A little discord; criticism of the conduct of others; or some grievance can easily become reason for leaving the church. No Christian can be joyful without the assistance of others who share his faith. That was the reason why God gave the command: "Forsake not the assembling of yourselves together" (Hebrews 10:25). Peter must have been very agitated. At one point during his testing he left the fire and actually reached the porch. "But he denied saying, I know not, neither understand I what thou sayest. And he went out into the porch, and the cock crew" (Mark 14:68). It was to be regretted that he did not continue his walk into the night. He was so near to deliverance, but unfortunately like Lot's wife, he looked back (see Genesis 19:26)!

Even in the midst of fierce temptation, God opens a way to victory, but alas, many people choose the fellowship at the fire instead of the walk beneath the stars. The Church, in spite of her blemishes, remains the best institution in the world. All the blessings of western civilization were brought to us by men and women who lay down their lives to share the glorious Gospel of the grace of God. The assembly of Christians is a family where depressed souls find warmth, sympathy, understanding and help. Without his brethren, Peter would have been a very lonely man. Encouraged by them he became a preacher who influenced the entire world.

The Sixth Mistake

"And about the space of one hour after another confidently affirmed, saying, Of a truth, this fellow also was with him: for he is a Galilean" (Luke 22:59).

Peter's resistance was now stretched to the limit; he had abandoned decency and renounced faith in Christ and His friends. Yet, he neither spoke nor acted as did the local people. Someone said: "You are not telling the truth. You claim to be one of us but your speech is different. You are a Galilean. You speak and act as they do. You are untruthful." Peter's objection suddenly crumbled, and the same voice which had said: "Thou art the Christ the Son of God," began to utter profanities. "Then began he to curse and to swear, saying, I know not the man and immediately the cock crew" (Matthew 26:74).

"And Peter remembered." The cockerel's cry in the pre-dawn was a signal for the removal of a curtain which revealed what transpired earlier. All the arrogance, self-assurance and boasting seemed to be magnified as the Lord's warning was amplified within his conscience. He believed himself to be a hypocrite, a shameful being, a liar. When instinctively he turned to see the Lord he trembled, for probably the eyes of the Master were filled with tears. "And Peter went out and wept *bitterly*."

Somewhere in a secluded corner of the city he sat and wept, and the darkness of the night could not compare with the gloom which filled his soul. He was a wretched man, a coward and unworthy of the company of decent men. He probably believed the Lord would never speak to him again, but he was mistaken. Did he remember all the Lord had said? "When thou art converted, *strengthen thy brethren*." Men and women who have fallen consider only their shame. The Savior sees what may still be possible through the grace of God. That explains why His hand reaches out to men and women in need.

22

PETER LOSES A FOOTRACE

"The first day of the week, cometh Mary Magdalene early, when it was yet dark unto the sepulchre, and seeth the stone taken away from the sepulchre. Then she runneth and cometh to Simon Peter and to the other disciples, whom Jesus loved, and saith unto them, They have taken away the Lord out of the sepulchre, and we know not where they have laid him. Peter therefore went forth, and that other disciple, and came to the sepulchre. So they ran both together: and the other disciple did outrun Peter, and came first to the sepulchre" (John 20:1–4).

It is difficult to place all the appearances of the resurrected Christ in their chronological order. The writers of the Gospels completed their manuscripts several years after the events took place, and their words express their personal viewpoints. For example, John states that Mary Magdalene came alone to the sepulchre and returned to tell Peter and John that robbers had desecrated the tomb of the Lord. Mark says Mary was accompanied by Mary, the mother of James and Salome, and that they saw a young man who said, "Christ is not here" (see Mark 16:5–6). To reconcile the varying points of view may not be difficult.

There exists the possibility that Magdalene came before dawn (John 20:1), and that later, having spoken to the two disciples, she returned to be joined by the other women. To remember all the details of that memorable morning may not have seemed important after years had elapsed. Then and now, the fact of supreme interest was that Jesus had risen triumphantly from the dead and Mary knew where Peter and John could be found. She had waited until certain restrictions had been removed, and hoping to find comfort at the grave of her Friend, "came when it was yet dark." Seeing the stone had been rolled away from the door of the tomb, she jumped to the conclusion that the Lord's body had been removed, but why anyone should do such a thing was beyond comprehension. She ran for help, and finding the two disciples said: "They have taken away the Lord out of the sepulchre, and we know not where they have laid him." The fact that she said *WE* know not where they have laid him" may provide a solution to the problem already mentioned. Peter, who had reservations about meeting the Lord, immediately ran to find out what had taken place. If grave robbers had to be challenged, he was the man for the job!

John also was ready for action, and was the first to arrive at the tomb in the garden. Standing outside and looking into the shadows, he was contemplating what action to take when Peter arrived, and as usual was a man of action.

"Then cometh Simon Peter following him, and went into the sepulchre, and saw the linen clothes lie. And the napkin that was about his head, not lying with the linen clothes, but wrapped together in a place by itself. Then went in also that other disciple, which came first to the sepulchre, and he saw, and believed" (John 20:6–8).

It is thought-provoking that two men who had shared everything in life should be so different in their conclusions regarding what they saw in the tomb of the Lord. John saw and believed (John 20:8). Simon Peter saw and wondered (Luke 24:12). When the men looked at the burial garments lying upon the stone floor, Peter was exceptionally interested but seemed puzzled and unable to understand what had happened to the Master's body. John gazed at the clothing, and suddenly an overwhelming awe flooded his soul. A strange and mystical warmth filled his being and he did not know whether to kneel and worship or run outside and shout for joy. He smiled and knew that angels not grave robbers had been there to announce news of the resurrection. The stone had been removed not to let people enter, but to reveal the King of Glory had left. When the two disciples emerged, Peter was nonplussed and worried, but John was elated; he seemed to be walking on air! Peter wondered, but John believed.

The Undisturbed Clothing

John never forgot that memorable morning. Long afterward he described how Peter went in and "seeth the linen clothes lie, and the napkin that was about his head, not lying with the linen clothes, but

122

wrapped together in a place by itself." Basically that was all the tomb contained. Perhaps the two men, Joseph of Arimathea and Nicodemus who carried the Lord's body to the tomb, left certain articles which they thought might be used later by women who came with spices. Apart from that possibility the tomb would have been empty. The disciples saw the linen garments but there was something about these wrappings which fascinated the believing John.

The body of the Lord had been specially wrapped according to custom; the linen bandages had been carefully wound around the body. The head wrappings had encircled the chin and head. Two explanations have been offered regarding those items of clothing. Evidently they were undisturbed. Some theologians suggest the garments were still in their convolutions; that is, the folds were in place, but had fallen flat when the supporting body of Jesus vacated the wrappings. John, so it is suggested, looked at those coverings and realized the impossibility of placing them in that precise position without support being underneath. Even the head apparel had subsided into a flat position as if a gentle hand had carefully pressed the linen into a new position.

Other people suggest that sometimes in the Middle East, a body is prepared for burial by being wrapped in linen soaked in a special solution. When this hardens, the body is protected as though by a suit of armor. This would not alter the fact that in a miraculous manner, the body of Jesus had escaped. John could have seen either of these two sights, and both would strengthen his faith. The Savior had left without disturbing His grave clothing, which seemed an impossibility. Simon Peter saw the same evidence but detected nothing. He had only eyesight; his friend possessed vision!

The Unconvinced Colleague

"It was Mary Magdalene, and Joanna, and Mary the mother of James, and other women that were with them, which told these things unto the apostles. And their words seemed to them as idle tales, and they believed them not. Then arose Peter, and ran unto the sepulchre; and stooping down, he beheld the linen clothes laid by themselves, and departed, wondering in himself at that which was come to pass" (Luke 24:10–12).

The women whose names are mentioned were among the most faithful of the Lord's followers; the unnamed women were probably others who had followed the Master throughout His travels. Perhaps Luke was never told all the names of these people, but if he were, he considered the inclusion of their names unnecessary. The word translated "idle tales" is *leeros*. This according to Thayer means *nonsense*. Plummer states: ". . . the word is applied in medical language to the wild talk of the sick in delirium." The idea is therefore suggested that momentarily at least, the disciples considered these women to be emotionally unbalanced; a little sick in the mind; speaking words unsupported by fact. The fourth Gospel relates how two disciples ran to the sepulchre; Luke is content to speak only of Simon Peter. That Simon was there at all is something which deserves consideration. He had denied his Lord, and was very much ashamed of his own cowardice. It was difficult to face his brethren, but face them he did, and this proved his sincerity. When he arrived at the sepulchre to see the grave clothes lying in meticulous order, the sight filled him with amazement. John saw and believed; Peter could only see and wonder. When Peter had been somewhat arrogant, John had leaned on the Master's bosom; when Peter cursed, John had been keeping vigil. Dedication begat perception; self-assurance placed cataracts on the eyes of Peter's understanding. (Quoted from the author's commentary, *Luke's Thrilling Gospel*, Kregel Publications, Grand Rapids, Michigan.)

The Unparalleled Confidence

Peter and John were very different in temperament, outlook and thought. Both had been possessed of fiery natures, and John particularly was notorious as "a son of thunder." Yet John, by proximity to Christ, had absorbed something of the meditative loveliness of his Master. Anxiety and youthful energy brought him to the sepulchre; reverence and deep devotion stopped him at the sepulchre; and then worship, faith, and keen perception enabled him to see what less observant men would have missed. John was careful to indicate that they saw not the emptiness of the tomb, but the linen clothes and the napkin *wrapped together in a place by itself.* A. T. Pierson wrote, "'Wrapped together' fails to convey the true significance. The original means *rolled up*, and suggests that these clothes were lying in their original convolutions, as they had been tightly rolled up around our Lord's dead body. In John 19:44 it is recorded how they tightly wound—bound about—that body in the linen clothes; how tightly and rigidly may be inferred from the necessity of loosing Lazarus, even after miraculous power had raised up the dead body and given it life (John 11:44). This explains John 20:8—'*and John saw and believed.*' There was nothing in the mere fact of an empty tomb to compel belief in a miraculous resurrection; but when John saw on the floor of the supulchre, the long linen wrappings that had been so tightly wound about the body, and head lying undisturbed in their original convolutions, he knew that nothing but a miracle could have made it possible."

With loving care Joseph and Nicodemus had placed the Master's body on the slab within the rocky tomb, but at the appointed moment the Lord's body—glorified, transformed—rose through the wrappings and these in turn fell flat. Even the napkin by which the head had been circled and enclosed was in its special place. Neither friend nor foe could have arranged those garments in their meticulous order; the clothing itself bore testimony to the mighty hand of God. "And the angel answered and said unto the women, Fear not ye: for I know that ye seek Jesus, which was crucified. He is not here: for He is risen, as He said." Peter looked into the grave and *wondered*; his friend looked and *believed*. That one simple detail reflected the entire world. (Quoted from the author's commentary, *John's Wonderful Gospel*, Kregel Publications, Grand Rapids, Michigan.)

23

PETER RECEIVES AN UNEXPECTED VISITOR

"But go your way, tell his disciples and Peter that he goeth before you into Galilee; there shall ye see him, and he said unto you" (Mark 16:7).

"And they rose up the same hour, and returned to Jerusalem, and found the eleven gathered together, and them that were with them, Saying, The Lord hath risen indeed, and hath appeared to Simon" (Luke 24:33–34).

To appreciate this strange week in the life of Simon Peter it is necessary to understand the Savior was not crucified on the Friday of what has been called Holy Week. The whole of Christendom observes "Good Friday" as a commemorative day on which the Prince of Peace died for the sins of the world, but that deduction is incorrect. There is reason to believe the Lord died on Wednesday afternoon, and people who think otherwise misinterpret the Scriptures. The Bible teaches that Jesus rose from the dead on the first day of the week, the equivalent of our Sunday. It also states that His body was in the grave for three days and three nights (see Matthew 12:40). To make this possible He died on Wednesday afternoon. Sunset on Wednesday to the same time on Thursday would be one day and night. The same length of time to Friday would be the second day, and Saturday the third day. By this computation, Simon Peter denied the Lord on Tuesday evening. The Savior was beaten and accused throughout that terrible night; brought before Pilate on Wednesday morning; crucified at noonday and buried before sunset.

If, as the world has been taught, Jesus died on Friday afternoon and rose again on Sunday morning, the predictions concerning the death and resurrection of the Lord were incorrect. It is necessary to see these events in their proper perspective to understand Peter's experiences during that fateful week. The time in which he suffered anguish must have seemed endless.

Probably Simon last saw the Lord on Tuesday night when, blinded by tears, he rushed from the judgment hall. The man was not mentioned again until after the resurrection. Where was he from Tuesday night until the following Sunday? The distraught disciple was ashamed of his conduct, and probably believed his sin was unpardonable. He desired to be alone, but physical needs would compel his return to friends; he could not be a hermit for the rest of his life. As far as is known his only refuge was in the home of John Mark, the place where the Last Supper was instituted, and the early Christians congregated. That was the only large residence in the city where followers of Christ would be welcome. Peter's shame was more or less tempered by the fact that the other disciples had also forsaken the Lord; they were as guilty as he. Sooner or later Simon reached that home, where in all probability others had already gathered. The moment of his arrival and what was said to his host and hostess remain unknown. Christ's impending resurrection was completely unexpected; there was no light at the end of their tunnel. As far as Peter was concerned his career had terminated; the future was bleak. His only course of action was a return to his fishing boat. None of his colleagues were surprised when he said: "I go a fishing."

Apparently the Big Fisherman was not at Calvary when the Lord died; all the disciples except one were conspicuous by their absence. John, who was there with Mary the mother of the Lord, was the only source from which the rest of the party could glean information. Quietly, he was able to describe what had taken place. When the Master needed them most they had deserted and disappointed Him. Language could never express their sorrow and regret—even His funeral had been arranged and his tomb donated by comparative strangers.

Travel movement was restricted because of laws relating to the Passover; journeys were forbidden except for people endeavoring to attend the festivities. Contact with death meant defilement and forfeiting of greatly valued privileges. There was little to do except reminisce. Journeys would be permitted after the feast, and some of the women earnestly awaited the arrival of the new week when they could visit the Lord's tomb. A dead Christ would be better than none at all. To their everlasting credit they came to the sepulchre when men stayed elsewhere.

"And [the women] entering into the sepulchre, they saw a young man sitting on the right side clothed in a long white garment; and they were affrighted. And he said unto them, Be not affrighted. Ye seek Jesus of Nazareth, which was crucified: he is risen; he is not here. Behold the place where they laid him. But go your way, tell his disciples AND PETER that he goeth before you into Galilee; there shall ye see him, as he said unto you" (Mark 16:5–7).

The Specific Message . . . *"And Peter"*

It should never be forgotten that Peter was a disciple. He had denied the Lord and brought shame upon himself, but he was still one of the followers of Christ. When the Savior said to the woman, "Tell my disciples" that included Simon Peter. When Jesus mentioned Peter by name it was a clear indication He desired to meet again the man who had denied Him. The Lord wanted to make absolutely sure that Simon received a special invitation. "Mary, please be sure to tell him. Do not forget." The Lord knew His friend was embarrassed, and desired to alleviate his pain. It is not known when the three women delivered their message. Perhaps Simon was with the other men who listened as one of the women said: "Peter, He specially mentioned you. He intends to meet you in Galilee."

Apparently that invitation was ignored. Peter was so ashamed and believed he was too unworthy to meet the Lord again. Maybe he said: "It is no use. I am not coming. After what I did, I could never stand in His presence. He told me what would happen but I was too foolish to listen. No, you can go but I am not." That kind of conversation must have taken place, for it became necessary for the Savior to search for his obstinate disciple. Jesus had to teach Peter that failures could become stepping stones by which men reach higher and greater achievements.

The Seeking Master . . . *"The Lord . . . Hath Appeared Unto Simon"*

Luke described how two disciples returning to their home in Emmaus, were joined by the Lord Who appeared *in another form* (see Mark 16:12). Eventually they invited Him to share a meal and "he was known unto them in the breaking of bread."

"And they rose up the same hour, and returned to Jerusalem,

128

and found the eleven gathered together, and them that were with them, Saying, The Lord is risen indeed, and hath appeared unto Simon. And they told what things were done in the way, and how he was known unto them in breaking of bread" (Luke 24:33–35).

The Lord had promised to meet His disciples in Galilee, but when the Emmaus travelers returned they discovered the brethren were still in Jerusalem and were aware that the Lord had appeared to Peter. Apparently he had ignored the Lord's invitation. It was necessary to make a special journey to find the reluctant friend. Peter was ashamed and had to be convinced that in spite of his mistakes he was still loved.

The Startled Man

Somewhere in the city Peter was alone with his thoughts. Whatever would he say if the Lord confronted him? It was all right for the women to be enthusiastic, but they had not made fools of themselves as he had. He probably shook his head and sighed. Then suddenly a gentle whisper said: "Hello, Peter," and turning around the startled disciple saw the Lord. "Simon, didn't you receive my message?" "Yes, Lord, but it is no use. I know it, and You know it; You will be better off without me." The Lord smiled and replied: "Peter, that is something I must decide, not you." And as they talked together, maybe even angels listened and smiled. The Good Shepherd had found another wandering sheep, and was returning it to the fold. It would be thrilling to know what was said during that conversation, but some things are best unrevealed. Even God knows how to keep secrets, and for that fact Christians should be grateful.

This encounter was a turning point in the life of Simon Peter; ever afterward he could reminisce and say: "Jesus came looking for me." He was still capable of error in judgment and conduct, but the memory of that special encounter never faded from his memory. He reached pinnacles of fame thought to be impossible and won victories for Christ which beggared description. Maybe at God's right hand, the Lord looked down and said: "I am glad I found him." For many people Simon Peter is the most loved of all the apostles; he relates to everybody. The devotion of John was admirable; the personal work of Andrew was commendable, but Simon Peter made so many mistakes, that it is easy to believe he belongs to our family!

24

PETER FISHING FOR THE LAST TIME

"Simon Peter saith unto them, I go a fishing. They say unto him, We also go with thee. They went forth, and entered into a ship immediately; and that night they caught nothing" (John 21:3).

All the evidence supplied by the Gospels indicate that Simon Peter was a man of action. Sometimes he was impetuous and unwise; occasionally he was courageous and commendable, but always, for better or for worse, Peter had to do something. It was difficult for him to be still not doing anything. This became evident after the resurrection of the Lord, when instead of waiting for the Master's instructions, Simon abruptly said: "I'm going fishing." The possibility that Jesus might have other plans never occurred to him. He wanted to go fishing and that was all that mattered. Peter was always a leader, and it was not a cause for amazement when the other men agreed to accompany him. They said: "We also go with thee." That night they caught nothing. Any servant of Christ who acts independently of his Lord deserves to fail whatever his project may be.

This is a story of seven men in a boat! The vessel must have been of considerable size to accommodate so many fishermen. Nevertheless, John speaks of "a little ship" (John 21:8). Perhaps when the larger vessel was anchored in deep water, the smaller boat was used for other purposes connected with their occupation. Matthew wrote:

> "Then the eleven disciples went away into Galilee, into a mountain where Jesus had appointed them" (Matthew 28:16).

The fact that only seven of the party went fishing might suggest the others preferred to remain on the hillside. If they had been instructed by Jesus to go into the mountain, they might have been reluctant to embark on an unauthorized mission. If that were the case they were wise men.

The Master on the Beach . . . *Watching*

> "But when the morning was come, Jesus stood on the shore:
> but the disciples knew not that it was Jesus" (John 21:4).

It will be remembered that Christ after His resurrection chose occasionally to withhold the power of recognition from His followers; that is, He came in disguise to teach great truth. It is a wonderful thing for the eyes of the downcast to fill with glad surprise. It is even more wonderful when after a night of fruitless toil, men suddenly discover their uselessness was foreordained by God to help achieve unprecedented victories. Even the darkest night has a glimmer of radiance when mariners believe Christ awaits them on the shores whither they journey (see Mark 16:12).

One wonders what the Lord thought as He watched the disappointed men returning to the shore. If they needed food for their colleagues they were possibly worried; if they went fishing for pleasure a night had been wasted. They last saw the Lord in Jerusalem, which was quite a distance away. Jesus might have walked all the way to Galilee, but He arrived in time to solve their problems. Actually, He never arrives too late and all Christians should remember that fact.

> "Then Jesus saith unto them, Children, have ye any meat? They
> answered him, No. And he said unto them, Cast the net on the
> right side of the ship, and ye shall find. They cast therefore,
> and now they were not able to draw it for the multitude of
> fishes" (John 21:5–6).

Christ seemed to be one of the fish merchants who came to the beach in order to buy directly from the fishermen. When His question echoed across the bay, Peter replied, "We haven't any. Tomorrow, we may have some." The Savior's answer, "Cast your net on the right side of the ship" presents problems. It is hard to understand how experienced men who had been to the recognized fishing grounds; men who had failed to catch one fish, should suddenly respond to a Stranger's invitation to throw their nets into shallow water. Let no reader misunderstand these remarks. The author firmly believes that Christ, the Son of God, could have prepared many fish just as He prepared a great fish to intercept Jonah's flight from God (Jonah 1:17). Nevertheless, Christ's ability to do this would not explain the fishermen's readiness to obey an apparently senseless command. It is probable that from His vantage point on the beach the Master saw the movements of a shoal of fish swimming around the bay. His echoing command "Cast the net on the right side of the ship, and ye shall find," made the fishermen look in that direction, and instantly they saw what He saw. Their frenzied endeavor to get the net over the side resulted in a great haul of fish. The indolence and bitter disappointment of the preceding hours were completely banished as they struggled to land their catch. If this assumption be correct, if Christ had indeed seen the direction in which the fish were swimming and realized they would pass on the *right* side of the ship, it is easily understood why He spoke as He did. Sometimes we look for His hand in the miraculous events of life. It is wiser and better to see His guidance in the ordinary episodes of daily routine; to see and appreciate His nearness when we think He is far away. We need to detect the unfolding of His plans in the little things of life; in the disappointments and failures by which we are constantly surrounded.

The Men in the Boat . . . *Wondering*

The listless disciples suddenly discovered new energy when they saw the fish disturbing the surface of the water and became instantly active. Their net was quickly filled to capacity. At first they thought little about the haul of fish, for they were elated with their good fortune, but when John said, "That is the Lord" and Peter jumped overboard, the other men were spellbound. When they came ashore they saw a fire of coals on which breakfast had been prepared, and heard Jesus saying "Come and dine."

> "As soon then as they were come to land, they saw a fire of coals there, and fish laid thereon, and bread. Jesus saith unto them, Bring of the fish which ye have now caught. Simon Peter went up, and drew the net to land full of great fishes, an hundred and fifty and three: and for all there were so many, yet was not the net broken" (vv. 9–11).

Had the Master caught the fish with His own line? Did the Lord Jesus kindle a fire, cook the fish, and carve the bread? These are questions all would like to ask. The breakfast on the beach was destined to become immortal in the memory of those present. The Lord was Host, Cook, Waiter, Friend, Teacher, and in every role

132

proved Himself to be an expert. Had Christ desired He could have caught sufficient fish to meet every requirement; to Him it was as easy to catch a multitude of fishes as it was to take one. He was content to supply the first helping of the meal. Afterward He asked for additional supplies in order to teach that in fishing for men He and the disciples would need to work in close harmony. "We are labourers together *with God.*" (1) He is quite able to catch His own fish. (2) He instructs His followers, how, where and when to cast their nets. (3) As they were destined to share what He had caught, He also desired to share their catch. Either ministered to the other. This is the ultimate in Christian experience. Possibly Peter's hurried swim to shore left him stranded and embarrassed on the beach; the Master's request provided the excuse to work off a little more of his energy.

A. W. Pink has an interesting comment on this part of the story. "Peter drew the net to land: how remarkable is this in view of what is said in John 21:6. 'They were not able to draw it for the multitude of fishes.'" Surely this indicates another important lesson in connection with service. What six men had been unable to do, one man now did. Peter was weaker than gossamer thread when he followed his Lord afar off but in His presence God's power came upon him. He was concerned about his future, his appetite, and his occupation. When he said, "I go a fishing," he expressed what was in his mind. Then a new concern begat exuberance and excitement; he dived into the sea and swam for the shore, only to feel strange and perhaps a little ill at ease as he stood alone with his Master. He who had failed so badly, desperately wanted to please the Lord, and this concern added strength to his arms as he hurried to pull the net ashore. John remembered it all, and probably smiled as he wrote his story. Peter, in spite of many faults, was a likable man. John liked him and so do we."

The Message at the Breakfast . . . *Wonderful*

"So when they had dined, Jesus saith to Simon Peter, Simon, son of Jonas, lovest thou me more than these? He saith unto him, Yea, Lord; thou knowest that I love thee. He saith unto him, Feed my lambs" (v. 15).

"When Christ entered into this discourse with Peter—it was after they had dined—He foresaw that what He had to say to Peter would give him some uneasiness. Peter was conscious that he had incurred the Master's displeasure, and could expect no other than to be up-braided with his ingratitude. Twice, if not thrice, he had seen his Master since His resurrection, and Christ said not a word to him about it. We may suppose Peter to be full of doubts upon what terms he stood with his Master; sometimes hoping the best, yet not without some fear. But now at length his Master puts him out of his pain" (Matthew Henry).

There can be no doubt that Christ carefully planned this entire episode. John 18:18 speaks about the *fire of coals* at which Peter denied the Lord; John recalled how the Master had kindled a similar fire. At first there was no need for the Savior to say anything; the fire was searing Peter's conscience. Formerly, the disciple sat with the Lord's enemies; here he sat with the Lord's people. There, he hungered and there was no food for a disciple's soul; here, he sat at the Lord's own table. There, his burning words of denial left a scar on his soul; here, his confession of love thrilled those who listened.

(1) Much interesting comment has been made regarding the meaning of "*more than these*." Some have thought Christ was asking if Peter's love superseded the love of the other brethren. "Simon, do you love Me more than John and the others love Me?" It is problematical whether this supplies the correct interpretation, as the question might have caused resentment in the hearts of the others had Peter's answer been in the affirmative.

(2) Others think Christ's question could be expressed: "Simon, do you love Me more than you love these brethren?" This question would have been easier to answer; it would not be an offense to the others to reply, "Yes, Lord, I do."

(3) "Than *these* . . . " A few commentators suggest Christ was pointing toward the unconsumed fish; that He was saying, "Simon, so quickly and so easily you went fishing. Simon, do you love Me more than you love to fish; that is, Simon, could you continue to leave your occupation and everything else, just to follow Me and do My will?" It is not wise to be dogmatic about the relative values of these suggestions; the important feature is that Christ must have preeminence in *all* things. We cannot ask Him to be second in any project.

The Greek words used in the passage to express "love" are not identical. The Lord asked, "Simon, do you LOVE Me with that deep devotion that a son would have for a father? Simon, do you really love ME?" But Peter was unable to forget the shame of his former failure, and replied, "Lord, I am very, very fond of Thee. You are my Friend, and within my heart is great affection for You." It should be understood that he said this not because he did not truly love Christ, but *rather because he was learning to love himself less.* The resulting commission to feed the lambs of Christ's flock did much to restore his confidence. It should be noticed that Peter was told to feed lambs. Sheep should be able to feed themselves!

"He saith to him again the second time, Simon, son of Jonas, lovest thou me? He saith unto him, Yea, Lord, thou knowest that I love thee. He saith unto him, Feed my sheep. He saith unto him the third time, Simon, son of Jonas, lovest thou me? Peter was grieved because he said unto him the third time, Lovest thou me? And he said unto him, Lord, thou knowest all things; thou knowest that I love thee. Jesus saith unto him, Feed my sheep" (vv. 16, 17).

"When the Lord asked the question the third time, He graciously used Peter's word, *phileis me*: "hast thou affection for me?" It is noteworthy that when our faith is too small to reach His level of sublimity, grace brings Him down to our level; otherwise we should die in despair. Three times Peter denied his Lord; three times the Master urged him to confess. Overwhelming fellowship with Christ is the only antidote for the haunting memories of past failure. (1) If Christ could give this commission to Peter, then the disciple's lapse had been pardoned. (2) If Christ could trust even the lambs of the flock to Simon's care, then the Great Shepherd had confidence in Peter even though the disciple had none in himself. (3) If the mature sheep were to be led into green pastures and beside still waters, then even Peter could expect help from the One whose far-reaching mercy had brought these sheep into the fellowship of the fold. Simon Peter received three things: (1) *Pardon for his soul.* The Master had not cast him off. (2) *Peace for his mind.* Christ still trusted him. (3) *Power for his service.* The protection of the sheep necessitated the continuing interest of the Good Shepherd" (copied from the author's commentary, *John's Wonderful Gospel*, Kregel Publications, Grand Rapids, Michigan).

25

PETER TOLD TO MIND HIS OWN BUSINESS

*"And Jesus said . . . When thou wast young, thou girdest thyself,
and walkedst whither thou wouldest, but when thou shalt be old,
thou shalt stretch forth thy hands, and another shall gird thee, and
carry thee whither thou wouldest not. . . . And when he [Jesus] had
spoken this, he saith unto him, Follow me. Then Peter, turning
about, seeth the disciple whom Jesus loved following; which also
leaned on his breast at supper, and said, Lord, which is he that
betrayeth thee? Peter seeing him, saith to Jesus: Lord, and what
shall this man do? Jesus saith unto him, If I will that he tarry till I
come, what is that to thee? Follow thou me" (John 21:18–22).*

The meal on the beach had ended; the disciples were about to
leave the shoreline. Simon Peter was a little uncomfortable, for
he had been questioned by the Savior while all the brethren listened.
For once in his life he desired to escape from the attention. His
disgraceful denial of the Master had been brought into the open, and
friends had been reminded of that terrible night. He knew this was
unavoidable, and that sooner or later something would be said concerning his conduct. The Lord and he had met a few times since the
resurrection, but nothing had been decided concerning the future; the
fateful discussion was only being postponed.

Was he forgiven or not? Could he still become a fisher of men as
Jesus had promised, or had he forfeited the right to become the
Master's special evangelist? Would the brethren be able to forget
what had transpired and accept such leadership he was able to offer?
These questions refused to remain unanswered, and something had
to be done to restore Peter's confidence.

Now it was over; the unavoidable had happened, and Simon, although embarrassed, felt a little better. Yet, when the other men saw
him and then quickly looked elsewhere, the self-conscious disciple
became concerned. Their attention had to be diverted from him.

Jesus had spoken ominous words predicting that future problems would challenge Peter's faith. The disciples continued to talk about Peter and were forming opinions as to the meaning of the Master's words. Simon wanted them to speak about other topics, and seeing John approaching, asked the Lord: "What shall this man do?" Jesus probably understood what prompted the question and replied: "If I will that he tarry till I come, What is that to thee? Follow thou me" (see John 21:21–22). The Savior's reply was exceedingly gracious. If Peter were seeking relief from embarrassment he found it, for hearing the words of the Savior, the disciples probably talked all that day about the possibility that John would never die. Many years later, the Beloved Disciple explained:

> "Then went this saying abroad among the brethren, that that disciple should not die, yet Jesus said not unto him, He shall not die, but if I will that he tarry till I come, what is that to thee?" (John 21:23).

The Gracious Acquiescence

When God decides to correct His children, love holds the rod! Any idea that God is some kind of an avenging monster is outrageous. He is too wise to make mistakes and too loving to be unkind. The reply given by the Lord to His questioning disciple deserves consideration. Peter was seeking a refuge from his shame and the condemnation of friends. The Savior recognized this problem, and provided what was necessary. He opened a mental highway along which the thoughts of the disciples were soon hurrying. Suddenly they were provided with a new topic of conversation, and Simon breathed a sigh of relief.

The Great Assistance

When this conversation took place, Peter had no idea what would happen in his immediate future. Had he known about his forthcoming orations before thousands of potential enemies, he might have fled. He would be completely unequal to the demands soon to be made upon him. Many years later when he reminisced, he recognized that although he had been God's instrument on that memorable occasion, the phenomenal success attending his efforts was due not to his brilliance but to the risen Savior Who had poured divine strength into human weakness. The Lord had said: "Follow Me," and that was precisely what Peter had done.

The Glorious Assurance

The Lord, in so many words, had said: "Peter, let me give you some advice. Whatever may happen to your brethren, keep your eyes on Me. Where I go, follow; what I do, copy; what I say, hear." Peter never forgot the admonition, for when he was an old man he wrote: "For if ye do these things, ye shall never fall" (see 2 Peter 1:10). The words of the Savior were not only a command; they were an invitation. In spite of all that had happened the Master desired Peter's company. "Peter, stay close to me." If the disciple needed assurance of Christ's forgiving love, those words banished all doubt from his mind. Suddenly, the disciples ceased speaking about Peter; they had a new topic of conversation—John might never die!

The Gentle Admonition

"Peter, if I decide something, that is My business. What is that to thee? You are so prone to become involved with matters which are of no concern to you. That caused your downfall at the enemies' fire. You became involved in what other people thought and did. Had you minded your own business you would not have been burned!" That was how Simon would interpret the words of Jesus. Nevertheless, had another person said this to the disturbed disciple, the outcome could have been disastrous. Fiery words of condemnation might have devastated Peter, making him want to run away and hide.

When the apostle Paul sent a special request to the Christians in Corinth, he began his appeal in a significant manner. "Now I Paul myself, beseech you by the meekness and *gentleness* of Christ . . . " (2 Corinthians 10:1). It had been said of the Good Shepherd that He carried the lambs in His bosom—close to His heart. This fact was evident throughout His ministry. Hypocrites disturbed His serenity, but when confronted by people who were suffering, Christ's gentleness was as the Balm of Gilead. Sometimes fools rushed in where angels feared to tread, but the Lord was extremely careful when helping fallen souls to regain their balance and reach greater heights of achievement. Solomon was correct when he said: "A soft answer turneth away wrath but grievous words stir up anger" (Proverbs 15:1). Peter was still Peter; he continued to make mistakes, but throughout his career, whenever he thought of the Savior, something wonderful permeated his soul. Jesus had left behind a legacy of goodness, mercy, pity, and tenderness. The Lord had encouraged people to make a new start even when they felt like quitting.

Peter ... *Who Was Told to Mind His Own Business*

The nature of Simon Peter might have been described under three heads: (1) *He was very impulsive.* His fellow disciples hardly knew what to expect from the Big Fisherman, for while they soberly considered the pros and cons of a matter, their colleague enthusiastically pronounced a verdict. (2) *He was very inquisitive.* He was susceptible to the opinions of other people, and more often than not this led to trouble. (3) *He was very inflammable*; very temperamental. He could be alternately joyful and sad, inspired and carnal. Yet in spite of that fact, we all like Simon Peter.

A Dangerous Concern

The seaside breakfast had ended, and the disciples were watching the silvery waves move along the beach. Surging emotions filled their souls, for they realized that the stranger who had awaited the incoming boat was the Lord. It was wonderful to see Him as He gracefully sat watching the hungry men eating the meal He Himself had prepared. Tenderly, He had spoken to Peter and the thrice-asked question, "Lovest thou me," had stirred them deeply. Their colleague had been moved almost to tears, for the denials of an earlier occasion were still present in his mind. Then, after a while, Peter looked at John and said to Christ, "Lord, and what shall this man do? You tell me that when I am old another shall gird me and carry me whither I would not. Well, what about John? What will happen to him?" And the Lord answered, "If I will that he tarry till I come, what is that to thee? Simon Peter, your greatest mistake is that you are often looking at and thinking of other people. Do you remember how I sent you to take money from the mouth of the fish? You were upset then because other people's opinions overshadowed your outlook. Do you remember how you denied knowledge of Me? That happened because you permitted other people to influence you. Peter, be less concerned about other folk, and think more of your Master."

A Delightful Correction

"What is that to thee? If I be the Lord and you are My servant, your chief aim should be to do My will. If I decide that John should linger till I return, that is no business of yours, is it? Simon Peter, if you are to feed My lambs, and shepherd My sheep, you will need to look constantly to Me. The days ahead will be difficult, and if you lose sight of your Master, anything can happen. Therefore, do not be unduly inquisitive concerning John. Attend to your own affairs." Thus did Christ correct His disciple, and we all realize how necessary this had become. Even in after days Simon still permitted the opinions of others to sway his actions, and on one occasion Paul rebuked him because he compromised with the exponents of circumcision. Peter was always getting into trouble because he had not mastered the art of minding his own business (see Galatians 2:11–16).

A Definite Command

"Follow thou me." When Peter heard this command his thoughts probably went back to the morning when the Lord first called him, when, after borrowing Peter's boat, Christ said, "Follow me, and I will make you to become a fisher of men." Now, another commission had been given. He had been told to shepherd the flock of God. "Simon, follow me, for only thus will you succeed."

(1) *The follow-Me of Enlightenment*. The Christian pathway is beset with many dangers, and problems will arise to confound those who are not prepared for the emergencies of the way. "Follow Me, and you will learn of Me."

(2) *The follow-Me of Endeavor*. To follow Christ means to emulate His example. It means more than accompanying Him. When a soldier follows an officer into battle he does so to help his leader in the conflict ahead. To follow Christ means to fight for Him.

(3) *The follow-Me of Endurance*. "But when thou shalt be old, thou shalt stretch forth thy hands, and another shall gird thee, and carry thee whither thou wouldest not. This spake he, signifying by what death he should glorify God." Tradition asserts that Peter was crucified for his faith, that at his own request he was crucified head downward as he considered himself unworthy to die as did his Lord. Thus the fearful disciple who failed before the taunts of a servant girl, eventually reached unprecedented heights of personal loyalty. He followed His Lord to a cross; he was faithful unto death.

Some theologians think that John originally terminated his memoirs at the end of chapter 20; that the final chapter was an afterthought added at a later date. This might be true, but the consensus joyfully endorses the apostle's decision to add his postscript. Simon Peter's story belongs to all. At the beginning of the Gospel John reveals the power of the Lord in creation; at the end he tells of the grace of the Lord in redemption. He Who placed the stars in the sky also placed sinners in the Kingdom of God. He was the Son of God, the King of Israel—our Master!

26

PETER JUMPS THE GUN

"And in those days, Peter stood up in the midst of the disciples, and said . . . Wherefore of these men which have companied with us . . . must one be ordained to be a witness with us of his resurrection. And they appointed two, Joseph called Barsabas, who was surnamed Justus, and Matthias. . . . And they gave forth their lots; and the lot fell upon Matthias, and he was numbered with the eleven apostles" (see Acts 1:15–26).

The term "jumping the gun" is a modern expression used to describe someone whose impetuosity prevents a fair start to a race. It is used when an athlete begins to run before the official commencement of the contest. Then the entire procedure has to be repeated. This term fittingly describes Simon Peter who did something which was wrong. The Lord had returned to Heaven having instructed His apostles to tarry in Jerusalem and wait for the promise of the Holy Spirit, Who would superintend the growth and management of the Church. Unfortunately, Peter, who had assumed the leadership of the assembly, decided something had to be done to fill the vacancy caused by the treachery of Judas. As a result of his impatience, a lottery was arranged which, apparently, left God without a choice. A man named Matthias was chosen. Nothing had been heard of him during the ministry of the Lord, and as soon as he was appointed to high office he disappeared into obscurity. Simon Peter did not wait for the guidance of the Holy Spirit; he decided to go ahead with his own plans, and by so doing definitely jumped the gun!

Let it be admitted in all honesty that this was not in accordance with the command that they should tarry in Jerusalem and wait for the promise of the Father (see Acts 1:4). Led by the enthusiastic Simon Peter, the 120 people proceeded to arrange their lottery. First, they chose two of their brethren who were named Joseph and Matthias. It would appear from Peter's description of eligibility, that both Joseph and Matthias had been in or near the disciple group from the time John ministered in the Jordan Valley. To say the least, it seems strange that their names were never mentioned in the Gospels. They might have been among the seventy who were sent in pairs to proclaim the Gospel of the kingdom throughout the villages of Galilee. But if these men were of such outstanding ability that they were thought worthy of inclusion in the apostolic leadership, it appears strange that their talents, enthusiasm and devotion were never mentioned by any of the Gospel writers.

As we try to visualize that earliest of church meetings, the arranging to cast lots to vote either secretly or publicly on such an important matter boggles the mind! Their idea of casting lots left God with no alternative. One of the two nominees *had* to be God's choice. That situation brings to mind the day when Samuel was asked to choose one of Jesse's sons to become the king of Israel. Had they drawn lots in Jesse's home, the shepherd boy, David, would never have been brought in from the fields (see 1 Samuel 16:10–13). Peter and his associates did not wait for the guidance of the Holy Spirit, and there is reason to believe they made a great mistake. It is better to wait for the services of a competent guide than to run ahead and fall over a precipice! Matthias, as soon as he was elected, faded from the Bible story and eventually Peter also gradually ceased to be important. God found His own man to be the twelfth apostle, and the chosen instrument was Saul of Tarsus who became the apostle to the Gentiles.

Peter's Revelation Was Inconclusive

Apparently Simon Peter imposed his authority upon the infant church. He assumed leadership over the 120 people who had attended the prayer meeting which preceded the day of Pentecost. Three hundred and eighty people had left the company, but that did not supply evidence they had lost their enthusiasm or become unfaithful. Possibly many of those devout disciples had commitments which demanded attention; they went away to attend to legitimate duties. A hundred and twenty remained, but the continuing inactivity might have irritated Peter. As was to be expected he was a man of action, and standing before his colleagues said it was necessary to fill the vacancy which was caused by the treachery of Judas. It seems likely this was in accord with Hebrew tradition. There had been twelve tribes in Israel; the Savior had ordained twelve apostles, and Simon suggested this pattern should be preserved. He had evidently considered the matter and had studied Psalm 109:8 where David had spoken of an evil man whose days should be few, and whose "office" should be taken by another. As far as is known Simon did not consult the other apostles; he acted on his own initiative when he brought the matter before the assembly. There is nothing in David's psalm which suggests the procedure adopted by the early Christians. Peter believed action was necessary and that was all the encouragement he needed.

Peter's Remarks Were Ill-Advised

It seems strange that none of the other apostles reminded their colleague of the Master's command to wait for the Promise of the Father. Were they reluctant to oppose or reject his suggestion because they feared his fiery temperament? When the Lord instructed the disciples to await the coming of the Holy Spirit, He meant exactly what He said. Peter's suggestion was entirely unwarranted; he rushed in where angels feared to tread! The Christians who conformed to his ideas made a mistake. They listened to the advice of a man and ignored the command of the Master. This should be a warning to everybody. If a man quotes Scripture it does not prove his integrity. When God spoke from Heaven, He said: "This is my beloved Son: *hear Him*" (Luke 9:35). Never on any occasion did the Holy Spirit contradict anything spoken by the Savior. Christ had preeminence in all things, but Simon Peter believed he could solve his own problems. The idea of casting lots or registering a vote on such an important subject was ludicrous. The believers were asked to elect the man of *their choice*; it would have been wiser had they awaited the time when the Lord, by His Spirit, would make *His choice*.

Peter's Recommendation Was Interference

When the votes had been tabulated Peter announced that Matthias was the selected nominee, but the entire situation left much to be desired. One wonders what the reaction of the man who was not elected might have been. Was he hurt, disappointed or critical? Did he feel his service for Christ had been overlooked by the brethren? Did he feel like quitting? The answer to these questions may never be known. If any unpleasant repercussions troubled the church, the blame belonged to the apostle who was too impatient to wait for the guidance of the Holy Spirit. Dr. Luke described how the eleven apostles stood with Peter on the day of Pentecost and that means Matthias was among the official representatives of the risen Lord. That was to be expected, but it is equally important to recognize that Matthias was never mentioned again. The solitary appearance could hardly justify his becoming an apostle.

27

PETER'S FIRE ON HIS HEAD
AND IN HIS HEART

"And suddenly there came a sound from heaven as of a mighty rushing wind, and it filled all the house where they were sitting. And there appeared unto them cloven tongues like as of fire and it sat upon each of them. And they were all filled with the Holy Ghost, and began to speak with other tongues, as the Spirit gave them utterance" (Acts 2:2–4).

Historians reviewing the day of Pentecost could use the words of the late Sir Winston Churchill, by stating it was Simon Peter's finest hour! Only prophets could have predicted it; none could explain how it happened. All commentators agree it was accomplished because the Spirit of the living God took possession of an uneducated fisherman from Galilee. Let it be admitted that nothing in the Gospels suggests Peter was a great preacher; he never attended a theological seminary, and had not received training in the art of public speaking. As far as is known he had not delivered a major speech and was still the man accustomed to hauling nets on the Sea of Galilee. He could never become a student researching a subject about which he intended to speak.

With others he had been sent by the Lord to preach in the villages of Palestine, and had returned to say that devils had been expelled. Yet, it may be assumed that never in his life had he imagined addressing thousands of people who had rejected the claims of Christ. Observers would have agreed Simon Peter could not have accomplished what was done. Therefore, it is necessary to examine this remarkable occurrence. Everybody recognizes that Pentecost was an outpouring of the Holy Spirit when an ordinary man was given special ability.

The Prayer Meeting . . . *Searching!*

Perhaps the greatest characteristic about prayer is that *it changes the man who prays*! It is interesting to discover that each time the Lord was required to make an important decision, the preceding night was spent in communion with His Father. It is also important to know that every time the church has been revived, it was a definite answer to the prayer of devoted people. True revivals are never worked up; they are prayed down. It is very difficult for an impatient man to wait when his entire being yearns for action. Nevertheless sometimes God whispers "Be still, and know that I am God" (Psalm 46:10).

Obeying the Lord's command, 120 people who had witnessed the Master's ascension returned to Jerusalem to await the arrival of the Holy Spirit. Luke said that Peter and his friends "continued with one accord in prayer and supplication, with the women, and Mary the mother of Jesus, and with his brethren" (Acts 1:14). That prolonged period of intercession lasted for ten days, and indisputably, led to much heart-searching. Apparently it took time to remove self-interest from the thoughts of the early churchmen, but when that was accomplished they became filled with the power of God.

Dr. Graham Scroggie used to say: "It is easier to organize than to agonize. That fact has become evident in the modern church. Social gatherings, festivities, and other attractions will often fill a building, but God's benediction is given when dedicated men and women pray." The modern church is impotent because it has ignored the example given by the early Christians. When today's leaders need anything they appear on television hoping their appeal will reach sympathetic viewers. One wonders what would happen if they knew how to pray!

The Peculiar Method . . . *Startling!*

"And there appeared unto them cloven tongues like as of fire, and it sat upon each of them. And they were all filled with the Holy Ghost, and began to speak with other tongues as the Spirit gave them utterance" (Acts 2:3–4).

The signs attending the Pentecostal visitation were sensational. First, there came a sound which resembled a mighty rushing wind. A wind is never seen, but its effects are obvious. A gentle breeze may only disturb leaves on a tree, but a hurricane may demolish buildings. The ancient Hebrews associated the presence of God with "the going of the wind in the mulberry trees" (see 2 Samuel 5:24); it signified the Almighty was in the midst of His people. When the Holy Spirit came upon the believers, "it [He] filled all the house where they were sitting." Those who were there knew that they were in the presence of God. Then something strange happened.

"And there appeared unto them cloven tongues like as of fire, and it sat upon each of them." This had never happened before, and has not been repeated. The significance of this phenomenon has never been explained. No one can deny that it was a sign of God's approval and anointing for special service. Primarily, it was not evidence of believers being filled with the Holy Spirit. Since the day of Pentecost many outstanding Christians have been used by the Lord to accomplish things thought to be impossible, yet, and let it be emphasized, none of these saints ever appeared with a small flame resting upon their heads. That this happened at the feast of Pentecost suggests God has no favorites. The flame sat upon Simon Peter, and also the most insignificant souls in the company.

It should be remembered that when the Tabernacle was dedicated, the fire upon the altar was lit by God. When the apostles were anointed, evidence was forthcoming that this was the Lord's work and not the product of some organization. It is not known how long the flame stayed with the believers. If it were still there when Peter addressed the huge congregation, everybody would have recognized a special visitation from Jehovah. If it had disappeared, the memory of what had taken place supplied the inspiration needed to perform what had to be done.

It is significant that the language spoken by Peter so impressed the international audience, that they asked: "And how hear we every man in our own tongue, wherein we were born?" (see Acts 2:8). During any feast a multiplicity of languages could be heard in the city. Apparently Simon Peter did most of the preaching, for the Scriptures state the eleven disciples stood up with Peter (see Acts 2:14). It appears that the apostle used a language which everybody understood, and without which the Church could not have been established. Within a few days most of that international congregation would be on the way back to distant homes, and a priceless opportunity of spreading the Gospel would have been lost. The miracle of Pentecost, in its magnitude and effect, has never been repeated. If it had been, the task of missionaries would be easier—they would not have to learn a new language!

The Powerful Message . . . *Sensational!*

"Ye men of Israel, hear these words: Jesus of Nazareth, a man approved of God among you by miracles, and wonders and signs, which God did by him in the midst of you, as ye your-selves also know Him, being delivered by the determinate counsel and foreknowledge of God, ye have taken, and by wicked hands have crucified and slain. Whom God hath raised up, having loosed the pains of death; because it was not possible that he should be holden of it" (Acts 2:22–24).

Once again Simon Peter became the spokesman for the Lord, and the leader of his colleagues. Spontaneously, he answered the challenge of evil. With overwhelming conviction, he proclaimed they were witnesses that God had raised His Son from the dead. Quoting and expounding the Scriptures, Peter said: "Therefore let all the house of Israel know assuredly, that God hath made that same Jesus whom ye have crucified, both Lord and Christ" (Acts 2:36).

That meeting, which took place long ago, expressed four important facts. God was *watching*, *waiting*, *willing*, and *working*.

Watching

When the disciples believed their Leader had been abandoned God was observing every detail of what was taking place, and, instead of being indifferent, was "In Christ, reconciling the world unto himself" (see 2 Corinthians 5:19).

Waiting

God had heard every prayer, but if the Christians believed He was indifferent to their cause, they were mistaken. He was waiting for the moment when the day of Pentecost *had fully come*, and the complete dedication of His chosen servants. Peter did not try to become popular—he never desired the praise of men. He was the same person who hauled fishing nets on the Sea of Galilee, and was determined to present Christ as the Savior of the world. He preached what is now called "The Old-Time Gospel of Christ." God blessed it then, and has done so throughout the ages. Unfortunately, some sections of the church seem to have abandoned that kind of evangelism. Apparently, they are unaware that the only remedy for sin is the precious blood of Christ which was the theme of Peter's sermon. Paul was very wise when he instructed Timothy to "preach the word" (2 Timothy 4:2).

Willing

Perhaps some of the prayers offered by the early church were desperate; anxious people sometimes think God has to be coaxed or persuaded to respond to the needs of His children, that He is reluctant to do as His people desire. Men who pray should first examine themselves before asking the Lord to do something which might not be in accordance with His will.

Working

God is never idle. What happened at Pentecost exceeded the wildest dreams of the disciples. Probably the greatest lesson learned by those people was that all preachers should kneel before they enter a pulpit. It might be illuminating to ask what would have happened if Simon Peter had preached any other type of sermon. Charles Haddon Spurgeon, the great English preacher, often said: "It is not necessary to defend a lion; let it out of the cage, and it will defend itself!"

The Pre-Eminent Master . . . *Saving*

The greatest evidence for the effectiveness of the Gospel is the power that changes lives. One transformed soul is of more value than a thousand sermons. When a drunkard's home becomes a paradise, the critics are silenced. This became evident in the early church when some of the people who had consented to the crucifixion of Christ, repented of their son, and became ardent Christians. Their homes became a part of the Kingdom of God, and eventually they helped to evangelize the world. Peter and his friends would have appreciated the hymn which expresses all they believed:

> The head that once was crowned with thorns
> Is crowned with glory now.
> A royal diadem adorns
> The mighty Victor's brow.
>
> The highest place that Heaven affords
> Is His by sovereign right.
> The King of kings, and Lord of lords,
> And Heaven's eternal Light.

28

PETER WAS ASKED FOR ALMS AND GAVE FEET

"And a certain man lame from his mother's womb was carried, whom they laid daily at the gate of the temple which is called Beautiful, to ask alms of them that entered into the temple; Who seeing Peter and John about to go into the temple asked an alms. And Peter, fastening his eyes upon him with John, said, Look on us. . . . And Peter said, Silver and gold have I none; but such as I have give I thee: In the name of Jesus Christ of Nazareth rise up and walk" (Acts 3:2–6).

It must be remembered that the wonder and thrill of Pentecost were now things of the past. The little flames of fire were no longer visible on the heads of the disciples; they had been replaced by burning hearts. The experiences enjoyed in the Upper Room had terminated; the servants of Christ had returned to their ordinary world. When they considered what had taken place, they probably remembered their stay on the Mount of Transfiguration. There on the hillside the glory of God had reached down to touch them; the Master had been with them in most unusual circumstances. That they had desired to remain permanently on the mountain was not a cause for amazement; but, alas, the Master had brought them back into the valley where a father was waiting with his sick child. Pentecost surely revived memories of those hallowed moments. The coming of the Holy Spirit had brought them into contact with their ascended Lord; the joy had been indescribable; they could have remained in the Upper Room forever. Then the radiance diminished; the glow disappeared. As the father and son had waited for the Lord to return from the mountain, so a world was awaiting the coming of the disciples. When Peter, John, and the others left the Upper Room, they went through the doorway to face their greatest challenge. God had work for them to do; the tasks were in the valleys of life and not on the mountaintops of ecstasy.

"'Now Peter and John went up together into the temple at the hour of prayer, being the ninth hour'" (Acts 3:1). That these two men were together illustrates the unifying power of the love of God. Their friendship had commenced when they were fishermen at the Sea of Galilee, but the fact became obvious that in some senses they were opposites. Peter was a man of action; he was impulsive, sometimes thoughtless, and often mistaken in what he said, did and thought. John had been dominated by a fiery temperament but had mellowed dramatically. He had become a dreamer, tremendously devoted and patient. It might be said that either would have irritated the other; this had been manifested when the Lord invited the disciples to share the breakfast He had prepared on the beach (see John 21:20–22). In so many words Peter had been told to mind his own business, and not to be concerned with his brethren. For reasons unknown James had somehow temporarily dropped out of the picture. Peter and John were still together; probably either had discovered in his companion what appeared to be lacking in his own personality.

"It is interesting that they were going to the temple 'at the hour of prayer.' This was at nine o'clock in the morning; thirty minutes after the morning sacrifice. It is worthy of attention that the disciples were not present for the sacrifice; they came later to join with others as they knelt at the throne of grace. Peter and John were no longer interested in any offerings, but their desire to commune with the risen Lord would never diminish. Their message and mission were different, but their need would remain changeless. Without Christ they could do nothing. Prayer had become the way by which their spiritual resources could be replenished. This was the secret of the success enjoyed by the early church and has continued to be so in every spiritual awakening known throughout history" (copied from the author's commentary *The Amazing Acts*, Kregel Publications, Grand Rapids, Michigan).

To say the least, the story of the beggar who sat daily at the gate of the temple is interesting. It should not be assumed the man was poor; he might have been wealthy. Begging can be very lucrative, especially when generous people are entering or leaving a sanctuary. Even today the walkways leading to temples in eastern countries are lined with people soliciting gifts. The man who met Peter and John was carried each morning to his special place closest to the gate. Worshippers who entered the building passed within a few feet of the cripple, and since he had been afflicted from birth, he knew how to arouse their sympathy. It is not known if family or friends carried him each day, or if he paid helpers who also acted as bodyguards if other people coveted his favored place.

He was a man who lived on the outside. Perhaps he heard the singing of the Levitical choir, but had no desire to get closer to God's altar; he was perfectly content to stay where his business prospered. Perhaps occasionally an offering was given to the priests, but apparently the beggar had no desire for spiritual things; he liked being his own master where no one interfered. When he counted his money each night he smiled. His legs were useless, but it is an ill wind which blew no good!

When the beggar saw two men approaching he prepared to ask for help but had the shock of his life when one of the visitors said:

> "Silver and gold have I none; but such as I have, give I thee. In the name of Jesus Christ of Nazareth rise up and walk."

He was confused, for something was happening within his body. The stranger said: "Come on, get up and walk." The beggar surprised himself when he grasped the offered hand and jumped to his feet. He expected to fall, but his legs had become strong. Suddenly, throwing caution to the wind, he began jumping and praising God.

> "And all the people saw him walking and leaping and praising God. And they knew that it was he which sat for alms at the Beautiful gate of the temple. And they were filled with wonder and amazement at that which had happened to him" (Acts 3:9–10).

The healing of the beggar sent repercussions through the city. The temple authorities were annoyed, the citizens were elated, and the disciples strengthened in their faith. The miracle provided convincing evidence that the event was genuine, and not a figment of the imagination. Even the officials were compelled to admit it had truly happened. The man had lived for forty years and was known to thousands of people.

It has been recorded that the man's problems were in his feet and especially in his ankles. The Greek word translated "ankle bones" is *sphura* and is a most unusual word used in medical circles. It must be remembered that the author was a physician. Drawing attention to the suggestive medical term, Dr. Campbell Morgan in his commentary on *The Acts of the Apostles*, page 97, writes: "Immediately his feet and *ankle-bones* received strength. And he, leaping up, stood and walked . . . '" Perhaps only medical men can fully appreciate the meaning of these words; they are the peculiar, technical words of a medical man. The word translated "feet" is used only by Luke, and occurs nowhere else in the New Testament. It indicates his discrimination between different parts of the human foot. This particular word refers to the base, or heel. "*Ankle-bones*" is again a medical phrase, to be found nowhere else. The words "leaping up" describe the coming suddenly into the socket of something that was out of place; the articulation of a joint. This then is a very careful medical description of what happened in connection with this man. I asked one of my doctor friends, an expert in his own field, if he could explain the lame man's condition. He replied: "After years of suffering, the powerful flexor-tendons would have distorted the joint." He drew attention to a lame person trying to walk with a twisted, dragging foot where the toes seemingly had been pulled around toward the inside of the leg. He said: "A contracture would have developed to produce a malfunction of the joint. Walking and leaping would have been impossible without Divine intervention."

The charges brought against the apostles were groundless, and finally the accusers could do nothing except threaten additional reprisals unless they ceased preaching to the people.

His Content

"Silver and gold have I none." Peter's poverty for the most part was shared by many of the other Christians. Men had lost their employment, widows were without support, and the situation threatened to deteriorate even more. The necessity for assistance became evident. That some of the brethren were anxious to share their wealth deserves attention. The love of God had been shed abroad in their hearts. Property was sold and the proceeds placed in a central fund from which help was given to people in need. When Peter said: "Silver and gold have I none," he might have been stating his pockets were empty. Funds became available eventually, but at that moment the apostles were without money. This was a strange contrast to the Pharisees who always had small coins to give ostentatiously to encourage the praises of men. Peter and John had no desire to purchase popularity.

This lack of money was not alarming, for the apostles were

convinced the Savior would supply their needs. They preferred to preach rather than beg.

His Confidence

Peter's happiness was obvious; he possessed no money, but he had something of more value than the world's riches. "Such as I have, give I thee." The apostle never doubted his ability to meet the beggar's need. He had the power to perform the impossible, and could prove that some things were more important than money. We also have a commitment. What can we share with other people? Doctors have medical skill which may save lives; educators have knowledge to impart to students; counselors with training can help depressed people overcome their problems. What have we to give to people who need help?

Many years ago a crippled child attended a meeting where a minister was appealing for financial aid to erect a new church. He was startled when he saw on the returning collection plates a pair of crutches. Alfred, a disabled boy from the neighborhood, had no money to give, but he gave his crutches. They were sold to the highest bidder who returned them to the delighted lad. That sanctuary became known as Alfie's Church!

His Convert

Apparently the cripple never begged again; he had found a gold mine and was now leaping, and running, and praising the Lord. It has often been claimed that life begins at forty; this was certainly true of the crippled man (see Acts 4:22). It was not a surprise when the convert accompanied Peter and John as they entered the temple to pray, but plans were abruptly changed when Peter was given the opportunity to preach to a quickly-assembled congregation. It should be remembered the beggar remained with the apostles even when the priests became hostile. Evangelists are often asked if their converts STAND. Peter would have answered: "No, they go forward, leaping and praising God!"

His Claim

"Be it known unto you all, and to all the people of Israel, that by the name of Jesus Christ of Nazareth, whom ye crucified, whom God raised from the dead, even by him doth this man stand here before you whole" (Acts 4:10).

155

"And when they [the rulers of Israel] saw the boldness of Peter and John, and perceived that they were unlearned and ignorant men, they marveled and they took knowledge of them that they had been with Jesus. And beholding the man which was healed standing with them, they could say nothing against it" (see Acts 4:13–14). They could not understand how men from the fishing boats could confound lawyers employed by the Sanhedrin. Peter, a notorious coward, had become an accomplished orator, and it was impossible to refute his arguments. There was no explanation for this transformation except—that "he had been with Jesus."

There was no evidence to suggest that the fisherman had been a Bible student. Paul, who became the apostle to the Gentiles, had graduated from the Hebrew seminary where Gamaliel was president, but Simon Peter had only been with Jesus. Yet, to the amazement of the judges, he spoke of the prophets as if they were his brothers. It was difficult to challenge what he said, for like his Master he spoke with authority. It was frightening to know that what was being preached was affecting the entire nation, and it was impossible to predict where it would end. These men had to be silenced, but no one knew how to do it! Peter and John did not fear death, and sometimes seemed as if they would welcome it to be reunited with their Lord. When they were commanded to cease preaching their reply was challenging.

"But Peter and John answered and said unto them: Whether it be right in the sight of God to hearken unto you more than unto God, Judge ye. For we cannot but speak the things which we have seen and heard" (Acts 4:19–20).

Peter and John had gained their knowledge from the Prince of Teachers Who introduced them to Prophets, Priests, and Kings, and enabled them to understand the Word of God. Ultimately, they graduated with distinction from the Divine College to become accredited ambassadors of the King of kings. The Pharisees could not understand this phenomenon, but John Newton, who was once the captain of a slave ship, experienced a similar transformation when the grace of God changed his life, and helped him become a revered bishop of the Anglican Church. That remarkable clergyman wrote words which Simon Peter would have appreciated.

Jesus, the very thought of Thee
With sweetness fills my breast.
But sweeter far Thy face to see
And in Thy presence rest.

Jesus, my Shepherd, Savior, Friend,
My Prophet, Priest and King:
My Lord, my Life, my Way, my End,
Accept the praise I bring.

I would Thy boundless love proclaim
With every fleeting breath;
So shall the music of Thy Name
Refresh my soul in death.

29

PETER MEETS TWO PEOPLE WHO DIED BEFORE THEIR TIME

"But a certain man named Ananias with Sapphira his wife, sold a possession, And kept back part of the price, his wife also being privy to it, and brought a certain part, and laid it at the apostles' feet" (Acts 5:1–2).

Simon Peter was definitely the leader of the church during those early days. Some things are clear concerning the movements of the believers, but others remain unknown. At first the followers of the Savior met in the house with the large upper room; then they worshiped in a part of the temple known as Solomon's Porch. When the converts dramatically increased, other arrangements had to be made. Where the meetings were held and how they were conducted remain a mystery. Nothing was reported except that the saints were together and of one accord. When the need for financial aid became evident, believers who owned property sold their land and gave the proceeds to the apostles that people in need could be assisted. Among the generous donors was a man from Cyprus whose name was Barnabas. He later gained fame by becoming the friend and missionary companion of Paul.

The activities of such a large group of people commanded the attention of the entire country, and three facts became obvious. *Great power* attended the preaching of their message (Acts 4:33); *great grace* was upon the folk who shared their wealth (Acts 4:33); *great fear* fell upon the city when people began to realize how God detested hypocrisy (Acts 5:5). Perhaps the apostles still retained their headquarters at the house with the large upper room, for that was a suitable building until a permanent place could be found. It became necessary to elect a committee to superintend the distribution of aid, and as conditions improved, Peter apparently became the chairman of that select group.

"Neither was there any among them that lacked; for as many as were possessors of lands or houses sold them, and brought the prices of the things that were sold. And laid them down at the apostles' feet and distribution was made unto every man according as he had need" (Acts 4:34–35).

A Premeditated Plan . . . *Deception*

Ananias and his wife must have been interested in the project being sponsored by their friends. Everybody appeared to be helping impoverished Christians. The idea was marvelous and deserved support. One day, the married couple sat down to consider how to help. They possessed property, the income from which would be a safeguard against future need. Peter spoke about their land, so it seemed they owned sites suitable for houses or perhaps a small farm. They agreed it would be nice to participate in the project of the church, but their own needs could not be ignored. If financial problems arose they also might need to apply for relief. They had no wish to increase the burden being carried by the apostles! One of the two suggested it might be wise to give some of the money and keep the rest. They agreed that God helps those who help themselves. The idea of being penniless was not attractive. After the property was sold, Ananias brought what he thought was a fair share of the proceeds and placed it at Peter's feet. He explained he and his wife wished to help the needy. Had he explained this was only a part of what had been received, his gift would have been gratefully accepted, and in all probability Peter would have embraced him. The apostle inquired about the sale and was told he and his wife wished to donate all the money received for the property. It was their duty to help. Peter frowned and asked himself: "Why had the fellow told lies; why had he been untruthful to the Almighty?"

"But Peter said: Ananias, why has Satan filled thine heart to lie to the Holy Ghost, and to keep back part of the price of the land? Whiles it remained, was it not thine own? and after it was sold, was it not in thine own power? Why hast thou conceived this thing in thine heart? thou hast not lied unto men, but unto God. And Ananias hearing these words fell down, and gave up the ghost, and great fear came on all them that heard these things. And the young men arose, wound him up, and carried him out and buried him" (Acts 5:3–6).

A Perceiving Peter . . . *Disturbed*

Some people might criticize Simon Peter for what might be considered harsh treatment of two people who were trying to help the church. It must be remembered that the apostle did not kill the offending man and woman. Their death must be attributed to God, and before any complaint is made an investigation of the incident is necessary.

It might help to compare this event with the refusal to allow Moses to enter the Promised Land. It was a cherished dream of the patriarch to reach the land which flowed with milk and honey, yet, because he made one mistake, God denied that privilege. Nevertheless, a multitude of Israelites was permitted to enter in spite of the fact that they were completely unworthy. Moses made one mistake; they made thousands. The tribes enjoyed what their leader could not. Let it be admitted that occasionally it is difficult to appreciate the way God works.

Throughout their history when mothers told bedtime stories to their children, the favorite tale concerned the man who defied Pharaoh and brought God's people out of slavery. The eyes of the children filled with admiration as they listened, but when the parents told how Moses was forbidden to enter Canaan, the boys and girls were always surprised. Sadly the woman said: "He disobeyed God," and by that one act the entire nation learned the lesson of obedience.

Peter was confronted by a similar situation. The Lord was trying to instruct an immature people. If the early Christians knew how Ananias and Sapphira had tried to deceive the Lord and had escaped unpunished, others might have been tempted to emulate their examples. The death of the conspirators was probably the most effective lesson taught to the early church; it explained why great fear fell upon the people. Peter blamed Satan for the tragedy, but it was evident to all that God was not blind; He observed everything taking place, and detested hypocrisy. Every Christian knew it was better to please God and live, than to help oneself and die.

A Participating Partner . . . *Dying*

"And it was about the space of three hours after, when his wife, not knowing what was done, came in. And Peter answered unto her, Tell me whether ye sold the land for so much? And she said, Yea, for so much. Then Peter said unto her: How is it that ye have agreed together to tempt the Spirit of the Lord? Behold,

160

the feet of them which have buried thy husband are at the door, and shall carry thee out. Then fell she down straightway at his feet and yielded up the ghost. And the young men came in and found her dead, and carrying her forth, buried her by her husband. And great fear came upon all the church, and upon as many as heard these things" (Acts 5:7–11).

That the wife of Ananias came to Simon Peter three hours after the death of her husband suggests a question. Where had she been in the meantime? Since they had planned this escapade together, it would be assumed Sapphira would desire to share the praise expressed by the apostles. Had the woman been spending some of the money they had kept? Was she more concerned with shopping than with pleasing the Lord and helping people? Perhaps she was somewhat apprehensive fearing that their scheme might be discovered. Was it possible to deceive Peter who could be awesome and frightening? When asked a direct question concerning the sale of the land, she confirmed what her husband had said, and by so doing sealed her fate.

It was inevitable that news of the tragedy would circulate; suddenly fear fell upon the population. Everybody realized the foolishness of trying to deceive the chief officer of the church. If other men and women had been contemplating planning a similar error, they quickly changed their plans. Perhaps the dual tragedy saved the lives of many people. It also raised the standard of righteousness, and taught Christians to be honest in their commitment to the Savior. What is given sacrificially to Christ, in one way or another, is returned with interest; what is selfishly retained is easily lost.

A Practical Problem . . . *Demanding*

One of the most neglected doctrines of the Bible is the holiness of God. Unfortunately, many teachers omit to emphasize its importance because it condemns evil. Throughout the Old Testament dispensations, prophets emphasized that Jehovah was a holy God Who detested hypocrisy. Then Jesus came to reveal another aspect of the Almighty; He could be a heavenly Father awaiting the return of a prodigal son. Either message complemented the other, and both are necessary in the life of the Christian. Holiness and love were seen in the life of the Savior, and fully manifested when He died upon the cross. Solomon said: "The fear of the Lord is the beginning of wisdom" (Proverbs 9:10). The holiness of God did not make Him a monster, and the love of Christ did not make Jesus sentimental. Sin and righteousness do not walk hand in hand! That was the predominant lesson which the early Christians needed to learn. The Lord said: "Ye shall be holy for I am holy" (Leviticus 11:44). It is impossible to worship God and idols at the same time. The difference between the children of God and other people should be very obvious.

When the children of Israel left Egypt to begin their journey to Canaan, they were accompanied by a mixed multitude of people who became a constant source of irritation. Today, a similar situation exists in organized religion. Churches are supposed to be made up of Christians "called out" from the world and its systems, but many nominal members remain the same as they ever were. Anything is acceptable in their sight, they have no sense of sin, and no desire to become sanctified people. It was to prevent such a situation that God permitted judgment to fall upon two conspirators who practiced deceit. Ananias and Sapphira might have lived for many years, but they died before their time.

30

PETER UPSETS A PROMINENT CHURCH MEMBER

"But there was a certain man, called Simon, which beforetime in the same city used sorcery, and bewitched the people of Samaria, giving out that himself was some great one, to whom they all gave heed, from the least to the greatest, saying, This man is the great power of God. And to him they had regard, because that of long time he had bewitched them with sorceries. . . . Then Simon himself believed also: and when he was baptized, he continued with Philip, and wondered, beholding the miracles and signs which were done" (Acts 8:9–11, 13).

Only those privileged people who have lived through a spiritual awakening can appreciate what happened in Samaria when Philip the evangelist arrived to begin preaching the Gospel of Christ. When the late Rev. R. B. Jones was asked to describe what happened in Wales during the great revival in the years 1904–1905, he answered: *"God was everywhere!* In the mountains and valleys, in homes and streets, in the coal mines and shops, in the fields, the churches, yes, He was everywhere." That pastor could have been describing what happened in Samaria. Christ was everywhere; people were healed; meetings were crowded with excited people; educated rabbis and illiterate beggars were enthralled; families were united and blessed; cripples were healed; Jews and Samaritans forgot their racial bigotry, and through the love of God became brethren. Everybody knew the authorities were determined to silence the preacher and destroy his message but no one feared, for Jesus had risen from the dead and Philip was healing the sick. Every person in Samaria would have said "God was everywhere." What had happened in their city was becoming the talk of the country.

The Prominent Citizen

One man was genuinely disturbed. Simon the sorcerer had lost his influence over the people. He was the best-known man in the community; by combining deceit with artistry, he had perfected a system which captivated the entire community. He could tell fortunes, predict the future, give astonishing advice and solve problems. He was an expert in public relations, and quietly encouraged the people to believe he was God's representative. When honorable men passed him in the street they bowed in respect; if anyone were sick, Simon could always produce a remedy. Sometimes it was effective, but if not, he had other ways by which to solve their problems. Had he desired public office, he would have won any election. No man opposed him for he was a sorcerer, and enemies, so it was believed, could die prematurely! Witchdoctors in Africa exercise similar powers, but Simon was an expert at his trade; even the children were taught to respect and fear him.

When the Christians arrived in the city, the influence of the sorcerer was undermined for Philip never required payment for his services. Unimaginable blessings began to reach the people of Samaria, and everything was free. The young people of the city discovered a new hero, and Simon the sorcerer became a neglected man. His customers no longer sought aid, and he began to believe his business might be in jeopardy. Probably Simon was the only unhappy man in the entire city.

The Promising Convert

When the man saw crowds hurrying to hear Philip, he decided to seek the cause of all the excitement. He was amazed when miracles were performed and quickly realized they were beyond his comprehension. One night, he professed faith in the Savior and was publicly baptized. The converts rejoiced; they had won the most notorious sinner—with his money anything would become possible. The manifestations of God's power were so outstanding that a report of the work in Samaria reached Jerusalem, and the apostles, wishing to confirm the reports of unprecedented blessing, decided to send Peter and John to investigate the situation.

The news of the arrival of the two apostles stirred the imagination of the people, and the revival increased in intensity. It is interesting to note that Simon the sorcerer was *with* Philip. He stood beside him in the meetings. That may be very significant. When a prominent person arrives in any city, the civic authorities are never far away. Elected officials always accompany famous dignitaries in great auditoriums. It seems to be an effective way of winning votes on the eve of elections. The reputation and wealth of the sorcerer automatically gained for him a place at Philip's side; he was a good advertisement for the meetings; people were pleased to see him with the preacher.

When Peter and John arrived in Samaria, their presence brought additional prestige to the proceedings. They had walked with Jesus and were God's men. Their miracles were indisputable. Everybody was attentive to the message, but Simon the sorcerer was amazed and recognized something was missing in his own life. When Peter asked about the Holy Spirit, the people did not understand the question. The apostle placed his hands upon them and suddenly they also received their Pentecostal experience. The result startled and baffled the watching sorcerer. This was exciting! If he were able to perform similar miracles his influence would increase enormously. Maybe if Beelzebub were the chief of the devils, Simon could be the prince of sorcerers. If money could gain such distinction, Simon was willing to do business.

> "And when Simon saw that through laying on of the apostles' hands, the Holy Ghost was given, he offered them money, Saying, Give me also this power, that on whomsoever I lay hands, he may receive the Holy Ghost. But Peter said unto him, Thy money perish with thee, because thou hast thought the gift of God may be purchased with money" (Acts 8:18–20).

If the Samaritan believers were shocked by Peter's reply, they might have thought that since he was a newcomer to the meetings, he might have been unaware of earlier events. Maybe Philip should inform his colleague how Christ had changed the sorcerer's life! If the notable convert should be offended and leave the assembly, an inestimable loss might occur. But Peter was adamant, and said to the offending man, "Thou art in the bond of iniquity." Since Christians are said to be in Christ, it is difficult to avoid the conclusion that this man's profession had been false. He was still a lost soul who needed to repent of his sin. It was possible to belong—even to the early church—and still not belong to the Body of Christ. It is insufficient to be a member of any church if one's name is not written in the

Lamb's Book of Life (see Revelation 20:15). The following homily supplies additional information on this vital subject.

The Church Member Who Had Never Met Christ

Simon The Convert

Samaria was one of the first places where Christian enterprise overcame the hardships of persecution. When the church was driven from Jerusalem, the saints hastened to other places and began witnessing for their Lord. They did this in Samaria and great blessing immediately fell upon the new work. Led by the untiring Philip, the new evangelists preached the Gospel and revival began to change the city. People who had been enslaved to the wiles and sorceries of Simon, suddenly lost their fear and hurried to the meetings to hear of the risen Christ. The horrors of persecution were forgotten as men sought the Savior. Daily the church increased in size, and there was much rejoicing when the old sorcerer apparently saw his need of Christ, responded to the message, and publicly confessed his faith in baptism. Immediately he regained all the popularity he had been in danger of losing. The Samaritans considered it to be a matter for instant praise that their leading citizen unashamedly had joined their ranks. His coming gave added impetus to the movement, and within a short time the story of the revival in Samaria reached the apostles who had tarried in Jerusalem.

Simon the Covetous

"Now when the apostles which were at Jerusalem heard that Samaria had received the word of God, they sent unto them Peter and John: who, when they had come down, prayed for them, that they might receive the Holy Ghost" (Acts 8:14–15). The Christians were thrilled when they heard that two of the leading apostles were to continue the great work. The meetings were packed with eager, excited listeners, and all marveled when the new preachers demonstrated the power brought into their lives by the Holy Spirit. Simon the sorcerer was amazed when, through the laying on of the apostles' hands, the Holy Spirit was given to earnest seekers. But while other people in the congregation rejoiced and praised the Lord, the eyes of Simon looked hungrily toward the apostle Peter. Finally, he walked to the front and said, "Give me also this power, that on whomsoever I lay hands, he may receive the Holy Ghost" (Acts 8:19). His eyes lit with pride as he explained his ability to pay generously for the favor.

Simon the Condemned

"'But Peter said unto him, Thy money perish with thee . . . Thou hast neither part nor lot in this matter: for *thy heart is not right in the sight of God*. Repent therefore of this thy wickedness . . . for I perceive that thou art . . . *in the bond of iniquity*' (Acts 8:20–23). If any of the young Samaritan converts overheard Peter's remarks their courage might have failed, for such drastic treatment could easily result in the loss of a valuable church member. The apostle grimly uttered his words. The man was still in his sin—in the bond of iniquity. And since a Christian is never said to be 'in sin,' but rather 'in Christ,' here is the evidence that the sorcerer had never been saved. The man who had basked in the sunshine of men's favor suddenly realized the church had taken away his followers. He therefore made profession of faith in Christ and by so doing regained all he had lost. Yet, although he joined the church and was baptized before the people, neither his action nor the ordinance removed the stain from his soul. He was still a lost sinner, and Peter did not hesitate to say so. The man did not argue, but fearfully asked that prayer might be made on his behalf. Poor man! His church membership without a personal knowledge of Christ, was as empty as a body without life." (Reprinted from the author's book, *Bible Cameos*, Kregel Publications, Grand Rapids, Michigan.)

31

PETER MEETS A MAN WHO HAD
BEEN IN BED FOR EIGHT YEARS

---

*"And it came to pass, as Peter passed throughout all quarters, he
came down also to the saints which dwelt at Lydda. And there he
found a certain man named Aeneas, which had kept his bed eight
years, and was sick of the palsy. And Peter said unto him, Aeneas,
Jesus Christ maketh thee whole, arise, and make thy bed. And he
arose immediately. And all that dwelt at Lydda and Saron saw
him, and turned to the Lord" (Acts 9:32–35).*

Dr. Luke, who wrote The Acts of the Apostles, reported that
"Peter passed through all quarters." The apostle was endeavoring to catch men and women for Christ, and was doing the work
given to him by the Savior. During the course of his travels he came
to Lydda, which was described by Josephus as "a village not less
than a city." It was situated close to important highways which led
from Egypt to Jerusalem and Babylon. Evidently some of the dispersed Christians had settled in the vicinity and these gladly welcomed the apostle on his arrival. The area is best remembered for the
miracle performed on a man named Aeneas; the raising of the seamstress, Dorcas, and the hospitality given to Peter by a tanner named
Simon. The apostle stayed in his home for "many days." It would be
helpful if more information were available concerning Aeneas, who
had been bedridden for eight years. His name was of Grecian origin,
but whether he was a Jew or a Gentile was never revealed.

The Sick Man

"Palsy—or paralysis—occurs in scores of different forms. It may
be limited to a local area of the body, or be generalized. It may be
temporary or permanent. Almost everyone has experienced the temporary rigidity of ischemic palsy, due to interference with the flow of
blood to the muscles involved. Progressive, or wasting palsy, is seen

in muscular dystrophy with its gradual loss of muscular tissue. A striking example of generalized and usually permanent paralysis is seen in some cases of polio meningitis.

"The causes of palsy are many and varied. The condition may be inherited. It may be due to injury at birth. Sicknesses, such as polio or syphilis, may be responsible. A common cause is injury to a major nerve or to the spinal cord. Paralysis due to hysteria is seen occasionally. In Biblical days sins of an individual were blamed for his paralysis, and this thought must have added greatly to the patient's misery.

"Jesus cured people with paralysis (Matthew 4:24; 8:6; Mark 2:3). So also Peter (Acts 9:33, 34) and Philip, who cured many who were paralyzed" (Acts 8:7). (R. H. Pusma, *The Zondervan Pictorial Encyclopedia of the Bible*, Zondervan Publishing House, Grand Rapids, Michigan.)

The paralysis of the man in Lydda must have been one of the more serious kinds, for the Scriptures state he had been bedridden for eight years. It would be interesting to know how Peter *"found"* him! Since in all probability this was the apostle's first visit to the district, was the man discovered by chance or did some believing neighbor inform the apostle about the man and his condition? Perhaps some of his neighbors were filled with compassion and, hearing that Peter was in Lydda, asked him to visit the afflicted paralytic. It is not stated how the man was discovered, but when Peter said "Aeneas, Jesus Christ of Nazareth maketh thee whole," he responded immediately.

Apparently no personal request was made and nothing was ever said of Aeneas's subsequent actions. Did he join the local believers and become an effective witness for Christ, or did he fade into insignificance? It would be interesting to know that the remaining part of his life was given enthusiastically to the Savior.

If this interpretation has any substance, the unknown friends were like the four men who let a sick neighbor down through a roof so that he could meet the Savior. The next episode in the life of Peter concerns a seamstress named Dorcas, whose labors of love were known throughout the city of Joppa and whose friends did a remarkable thing.

"And forasmuch as Lydda was nigh to Joppa, and the disciples had heard that Peter was there, they sent unto him two men, desiring that he would not delay to come to them. Then Peter arose and went with them" (Acts 9:38-39).

Ordinary people can be successful soul winners even though they are not eloquent preachers. Many men and women have been helped because their friends cared sufficiently to tell a modern Peter of their special needs. When Christians make known their requests to God, there is no limit to what may be accomplished. After eight years of terrible suffering, the sick man at Lydda was miraculously restored to health and happiness because someone informed Simon Peter about his condition. This was a different kind of evangelism, but its effectiveness could not be denied.

The Strange Mandate ... "Arise and make thy bed"

This story is unique for it describes the only occasion in Scripture when a man was told to "make his bed." Elsewhere in the Gospels, one who had been healed was instructed to "take up thy bed and walk" (John 5:8). Aeneas was instructed to *make his bed*. There are two possible interpretations. Probably the man was in his own house and had no need to carry his bed—couch—or mattress to another place. Peter would know this, and therefore the emphasis was upon the rearranging of the bed to avoid further trouble. The Greek word used by Luke was *stroson*. He used a similar word in Luke 22:12, when he told how the Lord commissioned his disciples to prepare a place in which they could celebrate the Passover ("And he shall shew you a large upper room *furnished*" [*estromenon*]). Jesus knew that the place would be in order—already prepared. Peter therefore was advising the paralytic to set everything in its proper place, not to leave behind an untidy bed! It would be admirable to praise God in the streets, but it would be tragic if some person fell over disarranged bedding and broke a leg!

"Aeneas, you will never return to that bed of sickness, for Jesus Christ of Nazareth has made you whole; straighten the mattress before you leave it." Was Simon Peter at that moment bequeathing to posterity a truth everyone needs to learn? There are people who believe that conversion removes responsibility, but that is a misrepresentation of God's word. If a man be in debt when he becomes a Christian, his first obligation is to pay his debtors, put things in order. He should straighten his mattress, pay his debts, and not expect God to relieve him of responsibility. Making his bed was something which Aeneas was unable to do earlier. His new energy was evidence that something had happened to him—he had met Jesus of Nazareth.

The Stirring Movement

"And all that dwelt at Lydda and Saron saw him, and turned to the Lord" (Acts 9:35).

It has often been said that one miracle is worth thousands of sermons, and that was evident when the paralyzed man was healed. Peter was probably the most famous preacher of his generation. He had been the messenger of God at the Feast of Pentecost. Nevertheless, it was said that when the inhabitants of Lydda and Saron saw the healed man, they turned unto the Lord. There is no evidence that Peter preached to them; probably many of those people never met the apostle, but they did see the man who had been paralyzed, and that was sufficient evidence to prove Jesus Christ of Nazareth was alive.

Christ Lived

It was significant that Peter said: "Aeneas, Jesus Christ of Nazareth maketh thee whole." A dead Christ could do nothing! The apostle surely emphasized that when he said, in so many words, "It is not I who maketh thee whole. I can do nothing. Jesus only can heal you. You must never forget that fact. Men were paid to deny His resurrection, but let the critics take notice that the Savior is alive and well and is here to help you. The leaders of the nation can spend their money to support falsehoods, but let them understand what Jesus of Nazareth is about to do. Aeneas, arise and walk!" "And he arose immediately." Peter and the man from Lydda would have loved one of our songs.

> I serve a risen Savior, He's in the world today,
> I know that He is living whatever men may say.
> I see His hand of mercy, I hear His voice of cheer,
> And just the time I need Him, He's always near.
>
> He lives, He lives, Christ Jesus lives today.
> He walks with me and talks with me
> Along life's narrow way;

He lives, He lives, salvation to impart.
You ask me how I know He lives:
He lives within my heart.
                    —*Alfred H. Ackley, 1887*

Christ Loved

It must have been a thrilling moment when Peter knocked on the door and asked, "May I come in?" Aeneas looked up from his bed and could hardly believe his eyes. The famous preacher from Jerusalem had come to visit him; it was unbelievable. Later, when he reminisced he said: "He came because Jesus told him to come. Yes, Jesus cared enough to do that; He loved even a paralytic who had nothing to give in return. The Son of God sent His servant all the way to Lydda just to help me."

Christ Listens

Perhaps this was the greatest fact, for when the news spread through the locality, many people began to consider their own needs. Each time an anxious soul asked for help, the Lord Who had healed the man with the palsy, patiently listened. It might even be said that the influence of the healed man surpassed that of the apostle Peter. All the citizens of Lydda and the adjoining Saron trusted the Lord Jesus, and even the angels rejoiced when many precious souls began to love the Lord. That spiritual awakening not only stirred the population; it thrilled the heart of God.

32

PETER SPOKE TO A CORPSE THAT SAT UP

"Now there was at Joppa a certain disciple named Tabitha, which by interpretation is called Dorcas; this woman was full of good works and almsdeeds which she did. And it came to pass in those days, that she was sick, and died; whom when they had washed, they laid her in an upper chamber. And forasmuch as Lydda was nigh to Joppa, and the disciples had heard that Peter was there, they sent unto him two men, desiring him that he would not delay to come to them. Then Peter arose and went with them" (Acts 9:36–39).

Joppa was the ancient seaport of Jerusalem, and was situated about thirty to forty miles northwest of the capital city. It was famous in Jewish history, for through it Solomon brought the timber with which to build the temple (see 2 Chron. 2:16). It was also the port used by Jonah when he tried to run away from God (see Jonah 1:3). Obviously it was an important place, and therefore the Christians founded a church in the vicinity. One of its members was a lady named Tabitha, or Dorcas. The first name was Hebrew; the second Greek. But they both conveyed the meaning of gazelle—the beautiful antelope that roamed on the hills of Israel. It may or may not be safe to assume the lady was beautiful and graceful. Indisputably her character befitted her name, for her good deeds were known throughout the entire area. At that time the widows formed a distinctive part of every assembly, and it had become customary that these were helped from the common treasury (see Acts 6:1–4). Dorcas, who was a competent seamstress, devoted time, talent and energy to helping the needy ladies in her community. When she died her decease caused great sorrow, for her services were irreplaceable" (copied from the author's commentary, *The Amazing Acts*, Kregel Publishing House, Grand Rapids, Michigan).

The Concerned Church . . . *Desiring*

The believers in the village of Lydda were filled with sorrow, for one of their choice ladies had died. Dorcas, who was known throughout the area, had endeared herself to all the people who were aware of her services to the community. She ministered in a unique fashion as a skilled seamstress. Possibly Dorcas was a lady of means, for she apparently had no difficulty obtaining the material which she transformed into garments of great beauty. Her gracious ministry had won the admiration of everybody, but unfortunately, the lady succumbed to illness and left a vacancy which no other woman could fill. Many of the Christians were wondering how the fellowship could continue without her services. Some people preached with their lips, but she had won citizens with her needlework; she was an expert at her trade and an inspiration to everybody.

Later, the apostle Paul said to his friends in Corinth: "Ye are our epistle written in our hearts, known and read of all men" (see 2 Corinthians 3:2). Dorcas had been such a woman. Her life reflected the beauty of Christ; her deeds displayed the kindness of God, and her influence expanded in ever widening circles. Blessed are they who emulate her example. Amid the gloom and grief of the church, someone remembered that Simon Peter was only a few miles away and suggested he be asked to come immediately. It would be hard to decide what they expected from the apostle. Did they want him to preach an inspired sermon or hope he would raise to life their beloved sister? It is difficult to answer these questions, but at least they sent two men to interview their great leader. After the death and burial of John the Baptist, his disciples "went and told Jesus" (see Matthew 14:12). The believers in Lydda could not do that, but they did the next best thing; they told the leader of the church.

The Christlike Challenge . . . *Demanding*

It must be remembered that in spite of his God-given ability to heal the sick, Simon Peter had never raised the dead. The cripple at the gate of the temple had been healed, and further back when the apostle evangelized in the villages of Palestine, demons had been expelled, but raising the dead was something which only the Savior had accomplished. The challenge was now being presented: could Peter do what Christ had done?

When he arrived in Joppa, Simon Peter followed the example given by the Lord (see Luke 8:51–56). Evidently he was thinking of

174

that memorable occasion when Jesus expelled the professional mourners from the ruler's home. Probably he was thinking: "I had better
stay close to the Lord if I am to succeed in this mission." If a miracle
had not been forthcoming, he would have looked very foolish and
weak. Perhaps even the Savior looked down and wondered how far
His servant would go.

It is strange that some theologians deny the ability of Christ to
raise the dead. They affirm that the incidents mentioned in the Bible
describe people who were only in a coma. Peter, so it is claimed,
recognized this fact and merely awakened the woman. If the apostle
had been content with such a deliverance, the critics would still need
to explain the speed with which Dorcas was able to communicate
with her friends. Within moments she was grasping the hand of
Peter, and ready to resume contact with her Christian friends. It is
easier to accept the Scriptures than to believe the strange ideas of
teachers who are eloquent in explaining nothing!

The Considerable Commotion . . . *Disturbing*

"And all the widows stood by him weeping, and shewing the
coats and garments which Dorcas made, while she was with
them. But Peter put them all forth . . . " (Acts 9:39–40).

Peter remembered how the Lord had done this in the home of
Jairus (see Luke 8:52–54). It was customary for bereaved people to
hire professional mourners; the greater the display of phony grief,
the higher became the charge for services rendered. This probably
was not so in the home of Dorcas, but the commotion made by some
of the widows was just as frustrating. They were displaying the
garments which Dorcas had made, and every way he turned Simon
Peter was confronted by noisy women. Everybody was concerned
with what had been done; no one seemed interested in what the Lord
might still do.

Simon Peter probably remembered what Jesus did on a similar
occasion. Lifting his arms to gain attention, he said: "Sisters, I would
like you to leave the room. I cannot pray when you are all making
such a noise. Please leave." They appeared to be surprised, but when
women began to leave others followed, and eventually the door was
closed. Then the apostle sighed and knelt beside the bed. At last there
was stillness, and Peter began to sense the presence of the Lord. How
could he hear the voice of God when people were creating an uproar?

Perhaps he remembered the experience of Elijah when he was hiding in the mountain. The forces of nature had been overwhelming, but afterwards in the silence he heard the still small voice of Jehovah (see 1 Kings 19:9–13). Even the Savior deliberately went into the hillside to avoid being interrupted as He talked with His Father. His spiritual power was never allowed to diminish, and it was for similar reasons He said to His disciples: "Come ye apart and rest awhile." People who are too busy to pray, are too busy!

The Complete Cure . . . *Delighting*

". . . and turning him to the body [Peter] said: Tabitha, arise. And she opened her eyes, and when she saw Peter, she sat up. And he gave her his hand, and lifted her up, and when he had called the saints and widows, presented her alive" (Acts 9:40–41).

It was a thrilling moment when Dorcas responded to the command of Peter by opening her eyes. The prayer of the apostle had been answered. He held out his hand to assist, and when she stood alongside, Peter invited the waiting friends to enter the bedroom. People who have been raised from the deadness of sin need the help of brothers and sisters who love the Lord. Without fellowship even Christians can be lonely. Dorcas was able to resume her charitable work, but was immeasurably enriched by the knowledge that through her experience many of the inhabitants of Joppa "turned to the Lord." Paul wrote to his friends in Rome: "And we know that all things work together for good to them that love the Lord, to them who are the called according to his purpose" (see Romans 8:28).

The Continuing Company . . . *Displaying*

"And it came to pass that he [Simon Peter] tarried many days in Joppa with one Simon a tanner" (Acts 9:43).

This verse is perhaps the greatest in the chapter. Luke kept "the best wine until the last"! A tanner, a worker in skins of animals, was considered to be defiled and unclean by orthodox Jews. Such men were deprived of privileges in Israel, and were forced to practice their trade at certain well-defined distances from places of habitation. This probably was the reason why Simon the tanner lived *by the seaside*! Often the odor around the home of a tanner was unpleasant, and people objected to the pollution of the atmosphere caused by drying skins and other paraphernalia connected with the odious trade. It might be inferred that when Peter went to reside in this man's house, he had overcome the prejudices of Judaism, but this was not the case. As will be seen in the study of the next chapter, Peter was still reluctant to associate with anyone unacceptable to Israel. Obviously Simon was a Christian, and the spiritual bond existing between the apostle and the tradesman was strong enough to overcome manmade objections. It is believed Peter stayed several weeks or even months, and that he used the time to evangelize the district. It would appear that while Jerusalem remained his headquarters, the importance of the city was diminishing. The call of the Gentile world would become irresistible, and Peter, though still a very rigid Jew, was beginning to appreciate why Jesus said: "Go ye into all the world and preach the gospel to every creature" (Mark 16:15). Within a few years Jerusalem would be replaced by Antioch, and from that center missionaries would be dispatched to preach the Good News throughout the known world. It is more exciting to launch a boat and sail it than to let it rust and disintegrate within the confines of a safe harbor.

That Simon Peter was content to live amid such odious smells might be explained by the fact that as a fisherman he was accustomed to harbors, boats, and sometimes, rotting fish! What might have appalled city dwellers would pass unnoticed by men associated with the fishing industry. Furthermore, the odor around the house of the tanner would almost guarantee the seclusion which Peter desired. There he could prepare for forthcoming evangelistic itineraries. Later it will be discovered that Simon Peter was accompanied by his wife, but whether she was with him in Joppa is extremely doubtful. Perhaps she was still caring for her mother in Capernaum, and had not yet become her husband's traveling companion.

33

PETER'S EYES AND EARS OPENED

"And he [Peter] fell into a trance, and saw heaven opened, and a certain vessel descending unto him as it had been a great sheet knit at the four corners, and let down to the earth. Wherein were all manner of four footed beasts of the earth, and wild beasts, and creeping things, and fowls of the air. And there came a voice to him: Rise, Peter, kill, and eat. But Peter said: Not so, Lord: for I have never eaten anything that is common or unclean. And the voice spake unto him again the second time, What God hath cleansed, that call not thou common, This was done thrice, and the vessel was received up again into heaven" (Acts 10:10–16).

Simon Peter never forgot that he was a Jew. He was proud of his heritage, and looked with suspicion on anyone and everything which taught things contrary to his faith. He accepted gladly the news that God loved the entire world, but strenuously avoided action which annoyed Hebrews. Probably, it was this characteristic which finally rendered him unfit for the enormous task of world evangelism.

The Christian leaders were predominantly Jewish and questioned anything which suggested Gentile participation in church affairs. They resented interference with Hebrew traditions. There remained many men who were reluctant to admit uncircumcised Gentiles into the fellowship of the church, and fraternizing with such people was discouraged. The First Church Council (see Acts 15) was convened because a dispute regarding this issue had arisen. When rumors began to circulate that Simon Peter had visited the home of Cornelius, even the man of Pentecost encountered opposition from people who should have known better than to question his actions. The entire church believed that God loved the world, but some members considered His special favors were for Jews only.

This had always been Simon's weakness, and the episode about to be considered caused the apostle's significant loss of prestige. Unfortunately, the Big Fisherman underwent a deplorable loss of favor, and it quickly became evident that Paul had become the leader of church expansion. Peter gradually disappeared into obscurity while Paul preached the Gospel throughout the world. As will be considered in a later chapter of this book, eventually Paul confronted Peter "face to face" regarding compromising with opposing officials (see Galatians 2:11). Doubtless it was planned by God that Paul should become the spearhead of the church's attack on the citadels of evil. Peter, unfortunately, almost became a forgotten man. He retained a dwindling number of admirers to whom he wrote two epistles, but as John the Baptist said of Christ, so he could have spoken of Paul. "He must increase, but I must decrease" (see John 3:30). This story regarding Peter's inability to recognize the purposes of God supplies evidence that his heritage and preconceived ideas were beginning to hinder his usefulness.

Cornelius the Captain . . . *Peter Delayed*

David was correct when he said: "The steps of a good man are ordered by the Lord," but he could have extended his statement by adding: "The *stops* of a good man are also planned by the Almighty." It was written of Simon Peter that "he tarried many days in Joppa with one Simon a tanner" (Acts 9:42). The question might be asked: "How long did he stay?" God's answer would be "long enough!" The Lord was aware of the need of a very important Gentile, and Peter was directed to stay in Joppa until that man was safely in the kingdom of God.

"There was a certain man in Caesarea called Cornelius, a centurion of the band called the Italian band" (Acts 10:1). The name "Cornelius" is interesting because a very special event made it famous. Historical records describe that about the year 82 B.C., Cornelius Sulla liberated ten thousand slaves, and all of these took their liberator's name to begin their new life. It is possible that the captain at Caesarea was a descendant of one of those emancipated slaves. He joined the army and became the leader of the tenth part of a Roman legion. The fact that his company was called "the Italian band" was not unusual, for other groups also had identifying names. Some commentators state this particular company was composed of archers specially trained for duty; liberated men to whom Roman citizenship had been granted. That they were stationed at Caesarea provides no problem since Herod the Great, in courting favor from Rome, had transformed a very difficult and dangerous harbor into one of the best havens along the Mediterranean coast.

Caesarea had been an inconspicuous village, but Herod made it his capital city. The problem of obtaining water supplies had been overcome when the king built a lengthy aqueduct that brought water from hills seventeen miles away. The large, brick arches that carried the supplies are among the most fascinating attractions still to be seen in Israel. The special detachment of Roman soldiers was there for a twofold reason: to please Herod, and to act as guards should an enemy try to sabotage what had become indispensable to the welfare of the occupying forces. Cornelius was the captain of this important group of men.

"A devout man, and one that feared God with all his house, which gave much alms to the people, and prayed to God always" (Acts 10:2). Obviously this captain was different from other centurions in Caesar's army. He was no longer interested in idolatry. It is not known when this man renounced his idols; neither is it known if, or when he became monotheistic and subscribed to the worship practiced in Israel. He worshipped God but was not circumcised as were the Jews among whom he lived. The Hebrew teachers would have identified him as a man very near to the kingdom of God, but not in it! It is interesting to read "he gave alms to the people, and prayed to God always." His faith in Jehovah was expressed in compassion for other people. The apostle John would have been interested in this man, for he wrote: "But whoso hath this world's good, and seeth his brother have need, and shutteth up his bowels of compassion from him, how dwelleth the love of God in him?" (1 John 3:17). Cornelius was constantly in the spirit of prayer; that is, even as he went about his duties as a soldier God remained in his thoughts. That he lived what he believed exhibited the sincerity of his soul. Such people are never far from God, and He is never far from them.

Cornelius the Concerned . . . *Peter Desired*

Peter was called to become a fisher of men, and was about to make his greatest catch. However, the Lord knew he would never succeed in landing his "fish" unless he underwent a crash course in the art of fishing.

"And Peter went upon the housetop to pray about the sixth hour. And he became very hungry, and would have eaten. But while they made ready, he fell into a trance, and saw heaven opened . . . and a certain vessel descending unto him . . . wherein were all manner of fourfooted beasts of the earth and

180

wild beasts and creeping things, and fowls of the air. And there
came a voice to him, Rise, Peter; kill and eat" (Acts 10:9–13).

It is not known whether Simon Peter saw this in a dream, or in a
special vision which God enabled him to behold. Suddenly every
instinct in his being began to rebel, for he was being instructed to do
something which had been conscientiously avoided throughout his
entire life. Since childhood, in common with all Hebrew children he
had learned from the Book of Leviticus that certain foods were pro-
hibited, and now God appeared to be contradicting His own laws.
Peter's initial reaction to these confusing instructions was that of
shocked concern, and the Lord thought it necessary to repeat His
message a second and third time. This suggests the apostle—as the
title stated—had cataracts upon his eyes and plugs in his ears!

He was unable to see wisdom in God's command and detect significance in the strange events until the Lord said: "What God hath
cleansed, that call thou not common." Yet, even then "Peter doubted
in himself what this should mean." In spite of everything which had
taken place, the apostle remained mystified and unconvinced. If we
may be permitted to use mixed metaphors, he was skating on thin ice
and feared falling into boiling water! At that time he had no knowledge of Cornelius who needed the assistance of the apostle; who, in
spite of preconceived ideas, was required to play an important part in
the Gentile's conversion.

Cornelius the Caller ... *Peter Debating*

"Now while Peter doubted in himself what this vision which he
had seen should mean, behold, the men which were sent from
Cornelius had made enquiry for Simon's house, and stood before the gate" (Acts 10:17).

There are no errors in God's timetable; all His activities are completed as planned. He is never too late nor too soon. He arranged for
Peter to stay in Joppa until His purposes concerning Cornelius were
fulfilled. He arranged that vision of Simon to coincide with the visit
of the soldiers. Every detail of His plans fitted into what might be
described as "A jigsaw of redeeming grace." Even the obnoxious
odor surrounding the home of the tanner assisted the visitors. Probably there were many Simons residing in Joppa, but only one Simon
who was a tanner. When the soldiers asked for directions to his

home, they were probably told to make for the sea and then follow their noses! They did that, and arrived at the precise moment when the apostle was about to descend from the roof of the tanner's house.

The three visitors looked at the stranger and politely asked if a man named Peter lived in the house, and receiving an affirmative reply, prepared to explain the nature of their errand. Meanwhile the apostle instantly recognizing his visitors were Gentiles, wondered what was about to happen. Then he heard the Holy Spirit whispering:

> "Arise therefore, and get thee down, and go with them, doubting nothing; for I have sent them. Then Peter went down to the men which were sent unto him from Cornelius; and said, Behold I am he whom ye seek. What is the cause wherefore ye are come?" (Acts 10:20–21).

The apostle was very attentive while they told their story, and then because evening was approaching he invited the men to spend the night in the home of Simon the tanner. His invitation was gratefully accepted, but whether or not any of them slept remains doubtful. The visitors could not appreciate the smell of drying skins, and Peter could not understand what God had in store for him. Hurriedly he summoned some local Christians and, explaining his predicament, asked if they would accompany him when he left the following morning. He knew that unpleasant repercussions would follow his association with Gentiles; his brethren would surely criticize his fraternizing with a Roman who belonged to the nation oppressing God's people. He was an enemy, and Simon Peter desired to have reliable Jewish witnesses who would corroborate any explanation he might be expected to give to critical brethren.

He had no desire to go to Caesarea, and he had not abandoned his beliefs. He went because there appeared to be no alternative other than disobeying God. Peter was in a difficult situation and to his credit let it be said it was wonderful that he swallowed his pride and did as he was requested. Perhaps he remembered how Jonah, faced with a similar mission, tried to run away from God. Peter was no stranger to the sea, but had no wish to be caught in another of the Lord's terrifying storms. It is better to have wisdom in your brain than water in your boat! To change the simile, it is better to have a fence at the top of a precipice, than an ambulance at the bottom!

34

PETER PRESIDES AT THE BEGINNING OF THE FIRST GENTILE CHURCH

It was only a comparatively short journey from Joppa to Caesarea, but to Simon Peter it seemed like one to the end of the world. His mind was in turmoil, the future uncertain, and his friends were fearful of what awaited them in the home of the Gentile captain. What he considered on the journey was expressed clearly when he arrived.

> "Ye know how that it is an unlawful thing for a man that is a Jew to keep company or come unto one of another nation; but God hath shewed me that I should not call any man common or unclean" (Acts 10:28).

Cornelius probably replied: "Yes, we understand your problem, but

> "Four days ago I was fasting until this hour; and at the ninth hour I prayed in my house, and, behold, a man stood before me in bright clothing. And said, Cornelius, thy prayer is heard, and thine alms are had in remembrance in the sight of God. Send therefore to Joppa, and call hither Simon, whose surname is Peter, he is lodged in the house of one Simon a tanner by the seaside, who, when he cometh, shall speak unto thee. Immediately therefore I sent to thee; and thou hast well done that thou art come. Now therefore are we all here present before God, to hear all things that are commanded thee of God" (Acts 10:30–33).

God's Preacher . . . *Responding*

The spacious residence of the Gentile captain was probably filled to capacity, for his family and friends had been summoned to hear Simon Peter. Luke wrote that Cornelius had called together his kinsmen and friends, and they had all responded. They knew the captain had abandoned his idolatry, but was constrained by an intense yearning to find reality in religion. According to Peter's statement they knew the facts of the Gospel, but did not comprehend how it related to them. The prophet had asked a very important question: "How shall they hear without a preacher?" If God loved all people, then no nation should be excluded from the fellowship of saints. Any man who considers himself superior to other children of God is not worthy of divine acceptance. Cliques and argumentative groups within the church are a menace, and unless they are removed or silenced, will ultimately divide the assembly.

God's Power . . . *Released*

As Peter explained how the Lord Jesus had provided salvation, the people sat enthralled, but suddenly, a remarkable thing happened.

> "While Peter yet spake these words, the Holy Spirit fell on all them that heard the word. And they of the circumcision who believed were astonished, as many as came with Peter, because that on the Gentiles also was poured out the gift of the Holy Ghost. For they heard them speak with tongues and magnify God . . . " (Acts 10:44–46).

The believing Hebrews who had come to Caesarea had difficulty believing what was seen and heard and had they not been present would have argued strenuously that it could not have happened.

The incident deserves attention, for the circumstances under which this event took place were different from those existing on the day of Pentecost. Peter did not have an international audience whose linguistic abilities were very diverse. The people in Caesarea probably spoke only two languages, their native tongue and Hebrew. The purpose behind this special outpouring was obvious. The Lord was not trying to evangelize the world, but was demonstrating that Gentiles were as precious in His sight as were the children of Abraham. The men accompanying Simon were able to testify later that he had nothing to do with the spontaneous outpouring at this mini-Pentecost. The Holy Spirit had interrupted the apostle's sermon and, without warning, had done for that small group what had been accomplished for a larger number at Jerusalem. The people did not speak with a strange tongue to explain the Gospel; Peter had already done that. However, the unyielding and perhaps stubborn Hebrews had difficulty believing Gentiles were equally as important to God as were Jews. As was to

184

be expected, Peter was severely criticized by his brethren in Jerusalem, but the testimony of the Jews who witnessed the event offset their accusations. When the Holy Spirit descended upon the Gentile believers, even the most hostile critic had to admit God was responsible for the manifestation. Thus, the first Gentile church was formed.

God's People . . . *Requesting*

"Then answered Peter, Can any man forbid water, that these should not be baptized, which have received the Holy Ghost as well as we? And he commanded them to be baptized in the name of the Lord. Then prayed they him to tarry certain days" (Acts 10:46–48).

It would be informative if we knew who did the baptizing. It seems evident that Peter did not. Did the accompanying Hebrew Christians from Joppa perform the ceremony? If not, then did the Gentiles baptize each other? Today, in many areas, only official representatives of an organized church are permitted to officiate at a baptismal service. This custom may add dignity and importance to the occasion but may not be a true interpretation of what was taught by the earliest leaders of the church. "Then prayed they him to tarry certain days" (Acts 10:48). Cornelius and his associates had tasted the manna from heaven and desired more. God had sent Peter to them; perhaps it would be possible for him to remain in their midst. We have not been informed of the length of Peter's stay in the centurion's home, but it is a safe assumption that the days were used for additional meetings when saints were taught more of the doctrines of grace. Thus did a *Gentile* assembly come into being; it was the first-fruits of a tremendous harvest. This was the initial example of "the church that is in their house" (see Romans 16:5).

HOMILY NO. 8

Cornelius . . . *Who Received a Strange Warning*

Cornelius was the most revered elder of his church, and chairman of most of its committees. Each Sabbath he bowed in the sacred house, and each weekday lived a life worthy of his noblest generosity. He was a target for every needy society. A man of integrity, he adorned his town, was an important member of the council, and was a very desirable friend. A person of bearing, breeding, culture, he was known and regarded by the highest officials in the nation, and his name was often mentioned in the society columns of the newspapers. He was certain of election to the Senate, but—reader, let me apologize. My mistake is inexcusable, my tenses have been confused. I should have said that Cornelius *would have become* such a man if he had belonged to a later generation.

He Was Good . . . *But He Was Not Saved*

"There was a certain man in Caesarea called Cornelius . . . a devout man, and one that feared God with all his house, which gave much alms to the people, and prayed to God always" (Acts 10:1–2). Cornelius was the kind of man who regularly studied the Scriptures and daily presided at morning and evening prayers. His sincerity was indisputable, and his influence extended throughout the town. He had few equals; yet, in the sight of God he was unsaved. He was certainly good according to moral standards, but he was not a Christian. When his servants interviewed Simon Peter they affirmed that their master had been *warned* by God to send for help. And when later Peter explained his conduct to the apostles, he stated that God had declared: "[Peter] shall tell thee words, whereby thou and thy house *shall be saved*" (Acts 11:14). Obviously then, good works plus a sincere religious belief are not sufficient to guarantee a man's salvation.

He Was Wise . . . *So He Did Not Argue*

There are many people in this world who are the exact replica of Cornelius except for one important detail. Whereas the man of old listened quietly to the suggestions of God's Spirit, his modern counterparts love to argue. Humility is the child of sincerity, and Cornelius was never seen to better advantage than when he bowed before God and His servant to hear the way of salvation. The fact that God *warned* this great man was truly suggestive. This was not advice; it was not merely instruction. Warning implies danger. The love of God embraced the entire world, but a man whose integrity equaled that of Cornelius attracted great attention. His very attitude demanded that God should bring to him the light of additional knowledge.

He Was Anxious . . . *So He Did Not Procrastinate*

"And when the angel which spake unto Cornelius was departed, he called two of his household servants, and a devout soldier of them that waited on him continually; And when he had declared all these things unto them, he sent them to Joppa" (Acts 10:7–8). If a warning revealed danger, then danger demanded action. This was a matter of paramount importance needing urgent attention. Other people might have decided to give the affair prolonged consideration; some could have shrugged their shoulders, dismissing this as a meaningless vision. Some might even have shared their thoughts with others and as a result would have been talked out of their intentions. Cornelius was a wise man. His sincere endeavors had failed to produce satisfaction. His piety only increased his desire for improvement, and as soon as God instructed him he took steps to obey the new commandments. His example might serve as our guiding star. Tomorrow is the most uncertain date on the calendar.

He Believed . . . *And He Was Not Ashamed*

"'The path of the just is as a shining light, that shineth more and more unto the perfect day' (Proverbs 4:18). When God revealed His acceptance of this Gentile soldier and his company, Peter marveled and said, 'Can any man forbid water, that these should not be baptized? . . . And he commanded them to be baptized in the name of the Lord. Then prayed they him to tarry certain days' (Acts 10:47–48). Cornelius was an officer in the Roman army of occupation. His baptism would invite attention in many places. However, since Christianity was considered an enemy of the State, serious repercussions could follow. Cornelius smiled and went ahead with his plans. He had found a new life and was not ashamed." (Reprinted from the author's book, *Bible Highways*, pp. 149–150, Kregel Publications, Grand Rapids, Michigan.)

35

PETER DEFENDS HIMSELF
BEFORE THE CRITICS IN JERUSALEM

"And the apostles and brethren that were in Judea heard that the Gentiles had received the word of God. And when Peter was come up to Jerusalem, they that were of the circumcision contended with him. Saying, Thou wentest in to men uncircumcised and didst eat with them" (Acts 11:1–3).

There is no evidence to prove that Simon Peter ever returned to the house of the tanner in Joppa. The length of his stay with Cornelius was never determined and we can only assume that since news travels fast, the conduct of the apostle was already being criticized when he was still in Caesarea. If Peter had become aware that his name was being slandered, it might explain why he bypassed Joppa and went directly to Jerusalem to prevent problems spreading within the church. He believed that a stitch in time might save nine! This episode in the life of Peter may appear to be unimportant, but it emphasizes certain essential facts. There are four propositions which challenge thought.

Proposition One . . . *It is always wise to think clearly before acting foolishly.*

People who act in haste usually repent at leisure! Men who perpetually drive too fast should reserve a hospital bed before commencing a journey! The apostle, Peter, was never known for his caution—he was the type of man who rushed in where angels feared to tread. The one exception to this rule took place in Joppa where, for once in his life, Peter did not act impulsively; he thought of the reactions which would follow his association with Gentiles. The apostle was aware of the attitude of some of his friends in Jerusalem, and had no wish to be involved in a dispute which could harm the church. Gossip would produce slander, and unless some reputable witnesses refuted the false insinuations, the unity of the church would be destroyed.

The apostle acted wisely when he sent for the leaders of the assembly in Joppa. Perhaps some of these men were known to the leaders in Jerusalem and their corroboration would be invaluable. Not all people would believe Peter's story, but if competent Hebrew Christians supported him, misunderstandings might be avoided. Perhaps Simon the tanner became Peter's messenger on that fateful night, and it was providential that the leaders of the church in Joppa consented to do as they were requested. Later, when the anticipated opposition became aggressive, the testimony of the men from Joppa averted serious difficulties. This simple investment of time and thought returned great dividends when Peter was accused of compromising with Gentiles.

Proposition Two . . . *It is never wise to make a judgment until all the evidence has been considered.*

When the news of Peter's conduct reached Jerusalem, even the apostles were surprised. After the initial report had been repeated five or six times, its accuracy became distorted. Simon seemed to be guilty of committing an unpardonable sin! People discussed his crime and, without knowing the facts of the incident, pronounced an innocent man guilty. Unfortunately this kind of thing continues to happen. It is regrettable that even within the church it is customary to condemn people for their mistakes, rather than to advertise their virtue. Deeds of kindness are expected and taken for granted; yet if someone makes a mistake, the error is continually remembered. This attitude is wrong, for men should be assumed innocent until proved guilty.

The story has been told of a man who was asked to accept an apology from a neighbor who had slandered him. He took the offender to the top of a hill and, shredding a newspaper, threw it into the wind. As these were blown away, the offended man said: "Go and collect all those pieces of paper." The fellow replied: "That is impossible." "Yes," replied the other man, "it is also difficult to undo the damage you have already done." Judgment should never be made concerning anything, or any person, until all the facts relevant to the case have been examined. That rule should have applied to Peter, but he was pronounced guilty even before the facts were considered.

Proposition Three . . . *A man who believes he is always right is frequently wrong!*

The hard heads in Jerusalem were convinced that their colleague had committed a great sin. He had done something in which they did not believe, and consequently could not be excused. Preconceived ideas warp the mind—men and movement which never make a mistake can be dangerous. The apostles were Hebrews who believed their interpretation of the law was infallible. They were convinced their utterances were always correct and reliable where contradicted Hebrew teaching was suspect and be denounced. If something went wrong it was always an error committed by other people! The Jewish leaders had been taught from infancy that Gentiles were unclean and should be avoided. The idea that the Almighty could love such people was considered to be ridiculous. Consequently, when the Lord began helping Gentiles His acts were accepted with reluctance, but when Peter and others began to treat aliens as friends, their actions appeared to be outrageous; they were inviting pigs to share their homes!

The critics never considered the possibility that even God could change His mind. His holiness was indisputable and sinners deserved punishment. Yet the same Jehovah Who warned guilty people pardoned repentant sinners. The same righteousness which condemned guilt could assist people in need. Circumcision was a physical sign that Hebrews were a separated people and different from aliens. Nevertheless, it was only a sign. When the Savior began His ministry, He provided a new concept of cleanliness. His sign was not produced by a knife, but by the Gospel which changed the lives of His followers. It was said, "If any man be in Christ, he is a new creature; old things are passed away; behold, all things are become new" (2 Corinthians 5:17). It was possible for an uncircumcised Gentile to be more pleasing to God than a circumcised Jew. It was also said: "The Lord seeth not as man seeth: for man looketh on the outward appearance, but the Lord looketh on the heart" (1 Samuel 16:7). This truth was never accepted by the leaders in Jerusalem, who preferred the old doctrines and were reluctant to accept anything new.

Propostion Four . . . *It is never wise to ignore a cancer in the hope it will go away.*

I knew a charming lady who belonged to a religious organization where the services of medical doctors were not desired. Her father was a leader in the movement, and his teaching destroyed the life of his daughter. She detected lumps in her breast, but to please her parent, refused the aid of a physician. Three years later that women was rushed to the hospital where she died. I attended her funeral, and believed a tragedy had taken place. Her life could have been saved had she responded earlier.

When Simon Peter heard of the situation in Jerusalem, he went to the city in an attempt to arrest something which could have become very serious. He did his utmost to remove a cancer before it claimed the life of the assembly. The apostle was not looking for a fight, and did not raise his voice and wave his arms; he was content to tell his side of the story. The storm subsided and peace was restored to God's people. What could have erupted into a very ugly situation was replaced by serenity, and everybody recognized that God knew exactly what was being done. It is better to hold out a hand to a potential friend than to make a fist and strike an enemy.

> "But Peter rehearsed the matter from the beginning, and expounded it by order unto them, saying, I was in the city of Joppa praying: and in a trance I saw a vision, A certain vessel descend, as it had been a great sheet, let down from heaven by four corners; and it came even to me: Upon the which when I had fastened mine eyes, I considered, and saw fourfooted beasts of the earth, and wild beasts, and creeping things, and fowls of the air. And I heard a voice saying unto me, Arise, Peter; slay and eat. But I said, Not so, Lord; for nothing common or unclean hath at any time entered into my mouth. But the voice answered me again from heaven, What God hath cleansed, that call not thou common. And this was done three times: and all were drawn up again into heaven" (Acts 11:4–10).

Some teachers express surprise that Luke should have included in his writings two accounts of this event. He described in chapter 10 all that transpired when God initially instructed Peter concerning the mission to be undertaken. The next chapter describes how Peter, in his defense, repeated all that had happened. Luke, who was a Gentile, emphasized God's purpose concerning all people and not only Jews. This command came from God and not from man. It was He Who first appeared to Cornelius, and everything that followed related to that event. Apart from the guidance of God, Peter had no excuse for visiting people considered unclean. If blame had to be apportioned, then the critics should blame God, for He alone was responsible for what had taken place. These verses may be considered under three headings.

Peter . . . *Challenged by Critics*

It is significant that the accusers challenged the apostle. Peter was not then what he has since been made, the vicegerent of the Almighty. Had he occupied that position, no dissenter would have questioned his authority. He was honored and loved among his brethren but never at any time did he claim to be superior to them, and never did they give to him a special place of honor. The apostle as he is now presented by certain sections of the church, bears no resemblance to the fisherman from Galilee. If he had been the spiritual head of the church, he might have replied: "Who are you to criticize me? Mind your own business! I did what God told me to do!"

Peter . . . *Careful but Confident*

Very carefully Peter rehearsed all that had happened in the homes at Joppa and Caesarea. He had no wish to antagonize his brethren, and yet he knew the necessity of preventing further trouble within the assembly. Solomon had said, "A word fitly spoken is like apples of gold in pictures of silver" (Proverbs 25:11). Peter's explanation at Jerusalem was a glorious example of that fact. The church was only in its infancy, and wounds had to be healed before they became festering sores endangering the health of the members. When Peter systematically told all that had transpired and that every movement had been suggested by the Lord Himself, he made his position impregnable. If modern Christians exercised the same restraint, many church problems would never arise.

Peter . . . *Convincing but Concerned*

It is not difficult to imagine Simon Peter slowly and almost laboriously reiterating each and every detail of his experience upon the housetop. He explained how he had seen the vision three times, and there was no possibility of misrepresenting what had transpired. The laws of Moses could not be abandoned; unfaithfulness would be reprehensible. God had repeated His command and finally repeated it again. Peter seemed to be saying, "Do not blame me; I had little to do with it. All you brethren should know that I had no power to bestow on anybody, Jew or Gentile, the gift of the Holy Spirit. Brethren, this is the Lord's doing, and it should be marvelous in our eyes." Even when Peter was making his defense he managed to hide behind God; there was not a safer hiding place.

36

PETER GOES FOR A WALK WITH AN ANGEL

"Now about that time Herod the king stretched forth his hands to vex certain of the church. And he killed James the brother of John with the sword. And because he saw it pleased the Jews, he proceeded further to take Peter also. . . . Peter therefore was kept in prison: but prayer was made without ceasing of the church unto God for him. And when Herod would have brought him forth, the same night Peter was sleeping between two soldiers, bound with two chains: and the keepers before the door kept the prison. And, behold, the angel of the Lord came upon him, and a light shined in the prison: and he smote Peter on the side, and raised him up, saying, Arise up quickly. And his chains fell off from his hands" (Acts 12:1–3 and 5–7).

The Unforgotten Simon

The church was in great trouble: James had been executed, Simon Peter was in prison and threatened with death, and the question was being asked among the disciples, "Who will be the next?" Some uninspired people would have been depressed, but that was not the experience of the early believers. Luke writes: "Peter therefore was kept in prison: *but* prayer was made without ceasing of the church unto God for him." It has been claimed "man's extremity is God's opportunity," and that thought must have been uppermost in the minds of the Christians. The outlook was forbidding and frightening, but the church could and did pray. This was a predominant feature throughout the writing of Luke's book; he emphasized the effectiveness of prayer in the lives of the apostles (see 1:14, 24; 2:42; 4:24–31; 6:4, 6; 9:40; 10:2, 4, 9, 31; 11:5; 13:3; 14:23; 16:25; 22:17; 28:8). The church did not possess armies with weapons. Compared with nations and kings, the Christians were powerless, but they could pray and say: "If God be for us, who can be against us?" Peter was secure in his prison, but the church knew God was expert at opening locked doors!

It was the normal procedure for a criminal to have two guards; but Herod, believing Peter to be dangerous, assigned a double guard so that escape would be impossible. It is significant that Peter was sleeping! Was he completely exhausted or relaxed? Perhaps he realized his times were in God's hands and that even Herod could be made helpless. Probably the apostle could have said:

> I cannot read His future plans,
> But this I know;
> I have the smiling of His face,
> And all the refuge of His grace,
> While here below. Enough! this covers all my wants,
> And so I rest.
> For what I cannot, He can see,
> And in His care I saved shall be
> Forever blest.

Luke said: "But prayer was made without ceasing . . ." The word translated "without ceasing" was *ektenees*, which according to Thayer means "to be stretched out; intentness of mind; earnest; assiduous." Literally, "the church was stretched out"—perhaps on their faces before the Lord. They were united in one purpose, to pray Peter out of prison. They could not use weapons but realized, as Paul later described, they "wrestled not against flesh and blood, but against principalities, against powers, against the rulers of the darkness of this world, against spiritual wickedness in high places." As a result, they prayed "with all prayer and supplication in the Spirit" (compare Ephesians 6:12 and 18). This was, and always will be, the secret of effective intercession. God promised that His people would find Him when they searched "with all their heart" (see Jeremiah 29:13). Real prayer grasps the hand of God and never lets go!

Peter slept between two soldiers, while the other men were guards outside the door (compare the notable event mentioned in Matthew 28:4 and ask, "Is anything too hard for God?"). Luke states that the angel smote Peter on the side. The Greek word used was *patazas*, from *patasso*, and it means "to strike gently." It is evident that Peter needed to be touched, shaken, or gently prodded. It is thought-provoking that the angel did not do Peter's work. God snapped the chains, but the prisoner was commanded to put on his sandals and cloak! There is a human responsibility in every answered prayer. We should never expect God to do our work. We are workers together *with* God, and nothing is impossible when we help each other. The Lord always does His best for us, but sometimes it is questionable whether we do likewise for Him.

The outlook was exceptionally gloomy when Simon Peter was imprisoned. James the brother of John had been killed, and to Peter, chained between two soldiers, escape appeared to be impossible. It was customary for prisoners to be shackled between two men, but Peter was considered to be a dangerous fanatic and additional men were assigned to his dungeon. Two were stationed at the door to prevent rescuers entering, and two others were inside to prevent the prisoner leaving.

The Feast of the Passover was about to be observed, and executions were not permitted for several days. Peter was therefore imprisoned with the prospect that as soon as the feast ended he also would forfeit his life. The Christians were aware of the situation; they could not resist Herod but they had access to the palace of the King of kings, and they prayed continuously for the release of their friend. The church at that moment was composed of *unbelieving believers*! They knew God could do anything, but when a maiden said Peter was standing at the door they thought she had taken leave of her senses.

The Merciless Monarch

"Herod killed James the brother of John with the sword" (Acts 12:1–2).

Herod was an astute politician who succeeded in charming even his enemies. Unable to oppose the armies of Rome, he concentrated on pleasing the emperor. He could not risk offending the Jews so scrupulously observed their laws and gained the admiration of people who otherwise would have detested him. He resembled a trapeze artist who skillfully walked a high wire without falling. Apparently he had no personal quarrel with the Christians, but when he perceived the Jewish officials were pleased by the execution of James he proceeded to take Peter also. That simple fact suggests a pertinent question. Why did God permit the death of James when his presence and guidance would have been of incalculable worth to the early church? It became evident that the life of Simon Peter was miraculously preserved—why was James allowed to die? Throughout the ages men have sought an explanation to that perplexing question, but a convincing answer has never been given.

Is it too much to believe that perhaps James was needed in Heaven? Was some special task awaiting his arrival, and did he receive a tumultuous welcome when he reached his eternal home? On the other hand, did his death accomplish more for his friends than would have been the case had he remained in their midst? Did the death of James compel the Christians to pray more effectively? When they could no longer receive his advice, did they lean more heavily upon the everlasting arms of their heavenly Father? There is reason to believe that some day we shall understand more clearly things which baffle us now; every unpleasant event will fit perfectly into the plan of God. The Bible states that God can make even the wrath of men to praise Him (see Psalm 76:10). It became evident to the church that Herod, after all, was not the Supreme Being. His fury could be, and was, restrained by the omnipotent hand of the Lord.

The Mistreated Minister

"And when Herod had apprehended Peter he put him in prison, and delivered him to four quarternions of soldiers to keep him, intending after Easter [Passover] to bring him forth to the people" (Acts 12:4).

It can only be imagined what Peter thought about the death of James, but when he was later chained to soldiers and thrust into the innermost dungeon, it seemed he would soon rejoin his friend in Heaven. That he slept between the soldiers suggests he was either exhausted or completely at ease knowing his future was in the hand of God. It was necessary for the angel to give him a "gentle push" and say: "Wake up. You and I are going for a little walk." The radiance of the heavenly visitor illuminated the cell, but it was amazing that neither the falling chains nor the conversation awakened the guards.

The Memorable Messenger

"And the angel said unto him, Gird thyself, and bind on thy sandals. And so he did. And he said unto him, Cast thy garment about thee and follow me. And he went out, and followed him; and wist not that it was true which was done by the angel; but thought he saw a vision" (Acts 12:8–9).

197

The angel of the Lord was seen—partially by Simon Peter, but sometimes God's messengers perform their miracles and depart unrecognized. The writer to the Hebrews said of the angels, "Are they not all ministering spirits, sent forth to minister for them who shall be heirs of salvation?" (Hebrews 1:14). Luke explained that Simon Peter *"came to himself"* (Acts 12:11), and that suggested the apostle had been dreaming. He walked along the street, and when the cold morning air played upon his eyes he began to consider his escape. It was interesting that the angel instructed Peter to put on his sandals and clothing. The feet needed to be protected, and the warm garments would prevent colds and possibly more serious ailments. It would have been tragic if the apostle had celebrated his deliverance by being stupid! Sanity can always be detected in the purposes of God. After Philip had baptized the Ethiopian eunuch, "the Spirit of the Lord caught away Philip . . . But Philip was found at Azotus" (see Acts 8:39–40). He was given a free ride to his next assignment. Peter was made to walk, and that provided time to recover from his trance.

The Mighty Miracle

"When they were passed the first and the second ward, they came unto the iron gate that leadeth unto the city *which opened to them of his own accord* and they went out and passed on through one street, and forthwith the angel departed from him" (Acts 12:10).

A Roman compound was always intensely fortified, and this was certainly true in Jerusalem where Gentiles were detested. The Jews were emotional and under great pressure, and could not be trusted to keep the peace. The outer gate which led to the city was made of iron—it could not be burned. This was the garrison's first line of defense, and was heavily guarded by men specially trained for the task. When it opened of its own accord it was evident God could effectively handle machinery. Had He desired, the walls and the gate could have fallen just as they did in the city of Jericho (see Joshua 6:20). When noise is essential, God can create it; when silence is required the actions of the Almighty can be as quiet as falling snowflakes.

Christians should never forget the Lord's ability to remove obstacles from the path of His people. When the children of Israel needed a road through the Red Sea, God divided the water and the tribes went over on dry ground (see Exodus 14:22). Peter believed he was having an exciting dream, but the night air quickly made him realize he was free! Perhaps had he not been in a trance he might have seen another angel sitting on the top of the opening gate! Suddenly he stood spellbound in the middle of the street; one moment he was following an angel and the next he was alone. Had he been hallucinating or was he actually free? Did he pinch himself to see if he were awake? Then he realized there had to be an explanation for what had happened. God had rescued him—but why?

"And when he had considered the thing, he came to the house of Mary, the mother of John, whose surname was Mark, where many were gathered together praying" (Acts 12:12).

Peter probably smiled; somebody had interceded on his behalf. There was only one residence large enough to accommodate many people, and instinctively the apostle turned in the direction of Mary's home. He knew he would be welcomed with open arms even although he arrived in the middle of the night. Without the fellowship of the saints he would have been a very lonely man—and so shall we if we become hermits!

37

PETER FINDS A HOUSE FILLED
WITH UNBELIEVING BELIEVERS

"And as Peter knocked at the door of the gate, a damsel came to hearken, named Rhoda. . . . And when she knew Peter's voice, she opened not the gate for gladness, but ran in, and told how Peter stood before the gate. And they said unto her, Thou art mad. But she constantly affirmed that it was even so. Then said they, It is his angel" (Acts 12:13–15).

It was in the early hours of the morning when Simon Peter knocked at the gate leading to the house of Mary. The continuing tapping seemed in the stillness of the night to resemble small explosions which threatened to awaken neighbors. The home of John Mark was crowded with Christians spending the entire night in prayer, asking the Lord to deliver Peter from the wrath of Herod. When the knocking was first heard, people began to wonder if the emissaries of the king had come to arrest them. As the visitor became more insistent, a maid, named Rhoda, fearfully approached the door wondering what she would say or do if enemies demanded entry. Suddenly she heard a whisper, "Open the door. Don't be afraid, It is I, Simon Peter; the Lord has brought me out of the prison. Please open this door." Momentarily, the surprised girl was paralyzed with gladness; she recognized Peter's voice and wanted to dance, sing and shout praises to God all in the same breath. Delirious with happiness, she ran into the house to tell her good news. The people stared silently at her, and then somebody said: "She is mad." When the servant girl insisted that Peter was standing outside, the unbelievers shook their heads and said: "It must be his ghost."

It is difficult to decide what that statement was meant to imply. Did they think Peter was already dead, and that his spirit had returned with a message of comfort? If Rhoda became annoyed with the faithless Christians she was justified. She might have replied: "I am only a servant girl but I am not stupid. I have heard that man many times, and I know his voice. He is standing at the door, and if you don't intend to let him come in, I will."

> "But Peter continued knocking, and when they had opened the door, and saw him, they were astonished. But he beckoning unto them with the hand to hold their peace, declared unto them how the Lord had brought him out of the prison. And he said: Go shew these things unto James and to the brethren. And he departed and went into another place" (Acts 12:16–17).

There are some vital facts here which invite investigation, but it might be wise first to consider:

HOMILY NO. 9

Peter . . . *Who Made up His Mind in a Hurry!*
Peter's Decision . . . When?

When Peter's mind became clear he knew a miracle had been performed on his behalf, and came to the conclusion this had not happened by chance. What had transpired was an answer to prayer and furthermore, if people were praying in the middle of the night they were together in some special place. It was only a matter of moments before he remembered the home of Mary, the mother of John Mark. Most theologians agree this was the home in which the Lord commemorated the Passover feast and which later became the unofficial meeting place of the early Christians. The descriptions supplied by Luke enable readers to visualize that spacious home. A small entrance door from the street opened into a courtyard at the end of which stood the dwelling. It was large and spacious and capable of accommodating the many who had gathered to pray. This delightful lady was a sister to Barnabas (see Colossians 4:10). Probably the family possessed great wealth. Barnabas had been able to give financial assistance to the early church (Acts 4:36–37), and his sister had the financial ability to own a large house and employ a household staff. The woman had courage, for it was dangerous to permit her home to be used by people who were being accused by the police and state rulers. Her action could have resulted in the confiscation of her property. Peter knew the home had become a sanctuary and within moments was hurrying to the meeting place.

Peter's Delay . . . Why?

"And as Peter knocked at the door of the gate a damsel came to hearken, named Rhoda. And when she knew Peter's voice, she opened not the gate for gladness, but ran in, and told how Peter stood before the gate" (Acts 12:13–14). James had been executed, Peter was in prison, and every Christian was in danger. Even the prayer meeting in the home of Mary could bring disaster upon the church. A knocking at the outer gate in the middle of the night was sufficient to cause alarm. Had an enemy betrayed the people within the home? It was the task of a servant to respond and to be careful in ascertaining the identity of the visitor. Did he come alone? Was he accompanied by others who had evil designs on the household? There was need for extreme caution. It is therefore easy to imagine the girl's questions: "Who are you, and what do you require?" That she was able to recognize Peter's voice testifies to the fact the apostle was not a stranger in the home; she had listened to him several times, and there could not be a mistake. Her mistress and the others had been praying earnestly for their preacher-friend and their prayer had been answered. Suddenly her heart filled with praise, and forgetting the man at the door, the servant ran through the courtyard to shout excitedly, "Mistress, Peter is here; he is knocking on the outer door." Had she been unaware of the identity of the visitor there would have been an excuse for her reluctance to open the door. Her delay was dangerous. Had enemies been following him, Peter could have been arrested.

Peter's Demand . . . What?

"But Peter continued knocking: and when they opened the door, and saw him, they were astonished. But he, beckoning unto them with the hand to hold their peace, declared unto them how the Lord had brought him out of prison. And he said, Go show these things unto James, and to the brethren" (Acts 12:16–17). It is difficult to understand the reluctance of those people to believe their prayers had been answered. They saw the immensity of the task but not the strength of God's hand. They believed the Lord could do what they requested, but had no faith that He would. The apparently hysterical cries of the servant suggested she had become deranged—overwrought—mad. When she repeated her statement, her hearers said, "It is his angel" (Acts 16:15). There was a common belief that all God's people had guardian angels who could, at any time, assume the appearance of those being protected. The men and women in the home of Mary therefore decided this had happened in the case of Peter, but the insistent knocking on the door challenged their decision. If the caller in the night were Peter's angel, then he was becoming a nuisance. If they did not respond quickly neighbors would soon be shouting protests. "And when they saw him, they were astonished." The stillness in the home was suddenly shattered by all kinds of exclamations. Then Peter raised his hand indicating he desired silence. He probably understood that the soldiers would soon be searching for the escapee; there was no time to lose. "Brothers and sisters, please be quiet. I want to tell you what happened." Then he said, "Go show these things unto James, and to the brethren" (v. 17). Evidently James and the other leaders of the church were absent. Were they in bed? Were they away preaching the Gospel? At that time of the night they were perhaps too tired to pray!

It is interesting to understand the command issued by Peter. He desired the local Christians to acquaint James with the details of his escape. Evidently this man was already being recognized as an outstanding church leader. It is generally agreed that he was the brother of the Lord, known as James the Less or James the Just. He swiftly came into prominence and presided over the first church council ever held (see Acts 15). Once again we are reminded of the fact that Simon Peter was not the earthly head of the church, and he would have been the first to deny he ever was. William Barclay says: "Now there is a certain mystery about this James. In the East it would have been the natural and the expected thing for the next brother to take on the work, and the task of an elder brother who had been killed. But from the story of the gospels we learn that Jesus' brothers did not believe on Him (John 7:5), and that they actually thought him to be mad (Mark 3:21). During the Lord's lifetime James was not a supporter of Jesus. But we learn that the Risen Christ made a special appearance to James (1 Corinthians 15:7). There is a very ancient work called *The Gospel to the Hebrews* which tells how, after the death of Jesus, James made a vow that he would neither eat nor drink until he saw Jesus again. It may well be that what the life of Jesus could not do, His death did do; that when James saw his brother die, he discovered Who He really was and dedicated all his life to serve Him. The change in James may well be another great example of the power of the Cross to change the lives of men" (William Barclay. *The Daily Study Bible. The Acts of the Apostles*, pp. 101–2). The rise of this man from obscurity to become the leader of the early church is a cause for amazement and gratitude.

"'And he departed, and went into another place' (v. 17). There was obvious need for haste and secrecy for Herod would be infuriated by the escape of his prisoner and would make every effort to recapture the escapee. It is intriguing that Luke, who wrote his manuscript many years later, did not mention Peter's secret destination. Did he consider it to be inconsequential, or was he unaware of the hiding place? The answer to that question may never be known. Roman Catholic theologians teach that Peter went to Rome and remained there for the next twenty-five years, but there is no proof this happened. Others think he went to the small towns near the coast such as Joppa and Sidon. Perhaps he went to Antioch, where the emissaries of Herod would have no authority. If this were the case, then Peter would be among Christian friends, most of whom were Gentiles. He would see for himself the continuing growth of the church and would remain there until the storm passed. Afterward he would continue his ministry in other areas." (Copied from the author's commentary, *The Amazing Acts*, Kregel Publications, Grand Rapids, Michigan.)

> "Now as soon as it was day, there was no small stir among the soldiers, what was become of Peter. And when Herod had sought for him, and found him not, he examined the keepers, and commanded that they should be put to death. And he went down from Judaea to Caesarea, and there abode" (Acts 12:18–19).

Herod could see no fault in himself and no good in others. Had he been a wiser man he might have known God was instrumental in arranging the escape of his prisoner. When the apostle had seemingly vanished into thin air and the guards could not explain his disappearance from the heavily guarded prison to hide his own infamy, the king ordered their execution and by so doing, hastened his demise. Within a very short time he fell from his throne and "was eaten of worms." He was dead before he died! When Simon Peter heard of Herod's death he probably said: "If God be for us, who can be against us?" If God ceases to strive with a man, doctors cannot help him.

Somewhere the wanted Christian was safely hidden, and even the most ardent search failed to reveal his haven. Peter eventually reappeared in Jerusalem where he addressed a meeting of elders. "Men and brethren, ye know how *that a good while ago* God made choice among us that the Gentiles by my mouth should hear the word of the gospel, and believe" (see Acts 15:7). It was evident that Peter had been away for a considerable time. When King Ahab sought in vain to find the prophet Elijah, God's servant was safely hidden. A similar thing happened to Simon Peter. The Lord led him to some safe place where enemies could not find him. The Psalmist was correct when he wrote: "He that dwelleth in the secret place of the Most High, shall abide under the shadow of the Almighty" (Psalm 91:1).

38

PETER TESTIFIES AT THE FIRST CHURCH COUNCIL

"And when there had been much disputing, Peter rose up, and said unto them, Men and brethren, ye know how that a good while ago, God made choice among us that the Gentiles, by my mouth, should hear the word of the gospel, and believe. And God which knoweth the hearts bare them witness, giving them the Holy Ghost, even as he did unto us" (Acts 15:7–8).

As far as is known, this was the first theological dispute within the church. It provided Simon Peter with the opportunity to make his last public appearance before the apostles. He was soon to disappear from the public eye, and, to his credit it must be said, he played an important role in making a critical decision. Paul and Barnabas had completed their first missionary journey, and everywhere great signs and wonders had confirmed their message. Nevertheless, they had encountered great opposition from legalists who maintained that without observance of the law, faith in Christ was meaningless. They believed Christians needed to be circumcised and adhere to the commandments of Moses. Their insistence on this procedure caused great concern and the believers were troubled. Paul vehemently opposed the teaching, and when conditions deteriorated it was thought necessary to appeal to the apostles in Jerusalem. Deputations from both sides of the conflict were dispatched, and all the representatives were ready to argue their cause. Simon Peter's presence indicated persecution had diminished; the apostle had emerged from his hiding place to attend what promised to be a lively session of the First Church Council.

It became evident to everybody that the church was on a collision course, and that unless some action were taken, the extension of the Kingdom of Christ would be in jeopardy. Circumstances demanded that competent judges should examine the pros and cons of the problem and pass judgment on an unavoidable issue. Probably at one of the regular meetings of the assembly, a decision was made that the apostles and elders should listen to both sides of the argument and then decide what advice should be given to the churches. Their decision would have repercussions throughout the world. The most effective way to study these Scriptures is to view the gathering as a meeting of the supreme court of the church.

It is not known whether this assembly was held in a building or outdoors. If we can assume it were indoors, there was disorder in the courtroom! The supreme court was in session; the revered leaders of the church were waiting to hear a case. A doctrine was to be tried but not the men who preached it. Even the opposition had the greatest respect for Paul and Barnabas, but they detested what they taught. Their spokesmen were ready to begin, but alas, there was too much noise among the spectators! People were arguing, and voices were raised throughout the courtroom. Peter, austere, determined, and observant, patiently waited for the hubbub to cease. What he had to say was important; he did not wish to waste time. "And . . . Peter rose up, and said unto them, Men and brethren . . . !" Suddenly, there was a great silence. Simon Peter had walked and talked with Jesus; even his stature commanded respect. The apostle's eyes surveyed the scene and, satisfied that he had gained the attention of everybody, he proceeded to express his thoughts.

His Claim . . . *God Made Choice—The Gentiles Should Hear and Believe*

There was an irrefutable fact. Peter had obeyed God's command to go to the home of Cornelius and there, with other representatives of the church at Joppa, had witnessed how God gave the Holy Spirit to Gentile converts. Yes, God had done something new; for even though the recipients were uncircumcised, He had bestowed His blessing upon them. It thus became evident that observing the law could not be a prerequisite to receiving the Holy Spirit. If that was not so, God had been wrong to do what He did. If observance of Mosaic law was essential to salvation, then the Lord should have commanded Cornelius and his household to do what was necessary, and afterward He would have told them what the next step should be. That God had bypassed legal requirements indicated He was revealing something completely new.

His Concern ... *Why Tempt Ye God?*

If God had refrained from imposing restrictions upon the seeking Gentiles, what authority had the Pharisees to demand Mosaic requirements? The law condemned; no man ever found peace through obeying its dictates; for even when sinners observed one commandment, they violated others. The fathers lived in constant dread, knowing they were incapable of performing the impossible. The innumerable requirements of Mosaic law had been a yoke on the necks of slaves; they were chains restricting freedom and evidence of helplessness and misery. The law demanded perfection, and this was beyond the reach of mortal man. Circumcision, the rite to be discussed, was only a small part of the law; to insist on observing that detail would be ludicrous unless equal emphasis be placed on the other requirements demanded by Moses. Therefore, anything that increased legal obligations was an infringement on God's prerogatives. Had He desired Gentiles to be circumcised He would have said so.

Peter's Conviction ... *"We believe that through the grace of the Lord Jesus Christ we shall be saved" (v. 11).*

Peter was careful to contrast conformity to law with faith in the living Christ. He opened the way for Barnabas and Paul to expound the doctrines of grace. Faith, not works, was the foundation upon which salvation rested. Men could be circumcised and obey the dictates of the law, but only Christ could cancel sin by the value of His atoning death. That was the Gospel given to Paul and he was so convinced of its authenticity that he later declared: "But though we, or an angel from heaven, preach any other gospel unto you than that which we have preached unto you, let him be accursed" (Galatians 1:8). Peter evidently had been impressed by what Paul had said during their confrontation and, by speaking in this manner, prepared the way for the missionaries to make their own statements.

Both Paul and Barnabas were convincing as they told of their exploits throughout the missionary journey, and the attention in the court was intense. It was significant that the presiding judge was James, the brother of the Lord. Simon Peter was not the chief justice; he was merely a witness who described how God instructed him to visit the home of Cornelius the Gentile. Claims that Peter was the head of the assemblies are false. He was soon to become a forgotten man, for the Gospel had been entrusted to Paul who preached it triumphantly to the end of his ministry.

James presided at that important session, and finally said: "Men and brethren, hearken unto me" (Acts 15:13). *"My sentence is that we trouble not them, which from among the Gentiles have turned unto God; but that we write unto them, that they abstain from pollution of idols, and from fornication, and from things strangled, and from blood. For Moses of old time hath in every city them that preach him, being read in the synagogues every Sabbath day"* (see Acts 15:19–21).

Sometime ago a leader of a professedly Christian organization criticized the decision made by James. He said: "He was wrong. Observance of the Mosaic law is necessary for salvation." It seemed strange that he considered the reconciling death of Christ insufficient to please the Almighty; it was necessary for sinners to add to the work of Christ. Thank God, *"IT IS FINISHED"* (see John 19:30).

Both Peter and Paul would have appreciated the words of P. P. Blish:

> Free from the law; Oh happy condition.
> Jesus hath bled and there is remission.
> Cursed by the law, and bruised by the Fall,
> Christ hath redeemed us once for all.

The closing part of Peter's life remains unknown. Tradition suggests that he traveled through many countries preaching the Gospel, and according to the writings of the historian, Origen, was crucified upside-down by the Romans because he believed he was unworthy to die as did the Lord. Some if not all of the suggested details may have foundation in fact, but as far as the Bible is concerned, Simon Peter was about to disappear from the record.

It is interesting to know how the leaders of the infant church made their decisions. Jerusalem was always a Jewish city, and it was not surprising when with the spread of the Gospel through Gentile countries, the headquarters of the church were transferred to Antioch from which missionaries were sent to evangelize the world (see Acts 13:1–3). Luke described in five different places, referred to responsible officials (see Acts 15:2, 4, 6, 22, 23). Twice he mentioned *the apostles and elders*; twice he wrote about *the apostles, the elders and the church*; and finally he spoke of *the apostles; the elders, and the brethren*. Simon Peter was an apostle who was always eligible to attend meetings where matters of concern were being discussed, but was only one of twelve men who met under the leadership of James, the brother of the Lord. These brethren were held in high esteem by the church, but they never desired nor encouraged absolute authority. They met with elders who presumably were brethren whose wisdom assisted in making correct decisions. These men represented all sections of the church; the apostles never became dictators!

Finally, Luke wrote of *the apostles, the elders and the brethren.* The five references already quoted indicate that church members were never excluded from business meetings. When a matter needed approval, the vote of the youngest member was as important as any other. Simon Peter was never what has since been claimed. He would have been extremely embarrassed if millions of people desired to kiss one of his big toes! At his best the apostle was a warm, lovable man who detested his mistakes. His final triumph came when he hung his head down from a Roman cross; it assured him of a tumultuous welcome in God's country!

39

PETER IS CRITICIZED BY PAUL

"But when Peter was come to Antioch, I withstood him to the face, because he was to be blamed. For before that certain came from James, he did eat with the Gentiles; but when they were come, he withdrew and separated himself fearing them which were of the circumcision. And the other Jews dissembled likewise with him; in so much that Barnabas also was carried away with their dissimulation" (Galatians 2:11–13).

The altercation which occurred between Peter and Paul has attracted the attention of the church in every age, but no scholar has ever determined when it took place. The sequence of events as supplied by Luke makes it difficult to ascertain when Simon Peter came to Antioch.

Either the apostles met "face to face" before the First Assembly was convened, or after the leaders of the church met in Jerusalem. It has been claimed the messengers from James arrived in Antioch long before the Council met, and that they were sent to remind Hebrew Christians of their responsibility not to offend pious Jews. Christianity did not supply a license to annoy other people. It has been suggested that prior to their arrival Peter had fraternized with Gentiles, and that subsequently, Paul's objections caused him to change his attitude and offer support when Paul argued his case at the Council. Others believe that since Barnabas was guilty of a similar offense, the confrontation took place *after* the missionaries argued over the reinstatement of the runaway nephew (see Acts 15:37–41). Paul would not have accepted as a partner a man who did not share his faith. The problem of when this event happened may never be settled to the satisfaction of everybody, but other details relative to the affair can now be considered.

There is no record of Paul's rebuke of Peter elsewhere in Scripture. It is a further proof of the apostle's independence as well as of his devotion to Christian liberty.

Consider The Conduct Of Peter

The Scene of This Interview between Peter and Paul—Antioch

It was a city on the Orontes, in Syria, the seat of the Macedonian empire in Asia, chiefly inhabited by Greeks, liberalized in thought by considerable culture. It was the second capital of Christianity, Jerusalem being the first, and held a prominent place as the center of Gentile Christian life. What occurred here would have wide results.

The Time

It occurred probably during the sojourn of Paul and Barnabas at Antioch, after the council of Jerusalem had settled the whole question of the relation between Jewish and Gentile Christians (Acts 15:30–40). Peter's conduct was, therefore, all the more singular and indefensible, because it was so necessary to secure Christian liberty on the basis of the decrees. We cannot forget that, long before, the vision from Heaven showed him the worthlessness of Jewish traditions (Acts 10:27).

The Circumstances

"Before that certain came from James, he was eating with the Gentiles; but when they were come, he withdrew and separated himself, fearing them of the circumcision." Those who came from James were not false brethren, nor even necessarily Judaic zealots, but certain persons whom he sent to Antioch, not to impose a yoke of ceremonies on the Gentiles, but to reassure Jewish Christians as to their right to observe the divinely appointed usages of their fathers, which the decrees of the Jerusalem council had done nothing to overthrow. The conduct of James was perfectly legitimate. Yet, it is probable they pleaded that there was no warrant in the decision of the council for the freer intercourse with Gentile Christians which Peter had been practicing. The Jewish Christians were still to "keep the customs," and not to mix freely with the Gentiles (Acts 15:19). When these persons came to Antioch, they found Peter eating with Gentiles as he had done before (Acts 10), disregarding the isolation established by Levitical laws. They found him, in fact, living as a Gentile, not as a Jew. Peter at once, through the influence of fear— probably the fear of losing his influence with the Jewish Christians— began to withdraw himself from the Gentiles, discontinuing his eating with them, without giving one word of explanation, and attaching himself to the Jewish Christians, as if the old distinctions of meats

212

were still in force and still sacred in his eyes. It is not said that the "certain from James" reproached him with his laxity. It may have been, after all, an empty fear on his part.

Its Effects upon Both Jews and Gentiles at Antioch

It involved the Jewish Christians in the hypocrisy of Peter himself. "And the other Jews dissembled likewise with him"—even those very persons who rejoiced at the decision of the council (Acts 15:31)" (quoted from *The Pulpit Commentary*. vol. 18. Wm. B. Eerdmans Publishing Company, Grand Rapids, Michigan).

Peter's Indiscretion . . . *Discriminating*

The apostle Peter, in the estimation of the Christians in Antioch, was a spiritual giant; he had walked and talked with the Lord; had been God's spokesman on the day of Pentecost, and his brotherly acceptance of Gentile Christians added luster to his reputation. The non-Jewish members of the church in Antioch adored the big fisherman, and many scholars believe he became the first bishop of the city. When he described how the Savior opened his eyes to see that all people were loved and recognized by the risen Christ, the Gentiles accepted him as a special friend.

When Paul and Barnabas were commissioned to become the first missionaries of the church, their departure meant that Simon was the only authoritative leader remaining in the fellowship. It was considered an honor to welcome him into the homes of the people, and hospitality was freely provided. If Peter had *not* been excited with his popularity, he would have been less than human! His hosts and hostesses were excellent listeners, and the apostle received so many invitations he had difficulty fitting them into his program.

One evening, someone mentioned that a special delegation had arrived bringing a message from James, the head of the church in Jerusalem. A strange silence fell upon the company, and even the apostle appeared to be preoccupied. What if the visitors returned to inform James about Peter's fraternizing with Gentiles and eating food considered to be unclean? What if the Jews resented his behavior and excluded him from their fellowship? If he became the center of a controversy, he would be of little use to Christ or the church. The nervousness of the apostle became increasingly obvious, and soon he asked to be excused. When he left the home he hurried away into the darkness, and there was no explanation for his departure.

When he began to pay attention to the Hebrews within the city, people became suspicious and soon even his friends whispered criticism of his behavior. Apparently, he had forgotten the words of Solomon: "The fear of man bringeth a snare, but whoso putteth his trust in the Lord shall be safe" (see Proverbs 29:25). Peter appeared ill at ease; he seemed to be living under a cloud! He avoided his former friends and paid more attention to the Hebrews. His influence began to wane; he was no longer admired.

Paul's Indignation . . . *Denouncing*

Paul heard of Peter's action and could hardly believe the report, but when its accuracy was established, his anger intensified. Had it been possible he would have confronted Simon Peter immediately, but for reasons unknown the apostle had left the city. Paul later explained to the Galatians: "When Peter was come to Antioch, I withstood him to the face, because he was to be blamed. . . . When I saw that they walked not uprightly according to the truth of the Gospel, I said unto Peter *before them all*, If thou, being a Jew, livest after the manner of the Gentiles, and not as do the Jews, why compellest thou the Gentiles to do as do the Jews? We who are Jews by nature, and not sinners of the Gentiles, knowing that a man is not justified by the works of the law, but by the faith of Jesus Christ" (Galatians 2:11, 14–16).

The indictment was exceptionally fierce for Paul resembled a bulldog—once he attacked something he never relinquished his hold! When Luke described the quarrel between Paul and Barnabas concerning the reinstatement of John Mark, he said: "And the contention was so sharp between them, that they departed asunder, the one from the other: and so Barnabas took Mark and departed unto Cyprus. And Paul chose Silas, and departed, being recommended by the brethren unto the grace of God" (see Acts 15:39–40).

Evidently Simon Peter had made a mistake, but Paul considered him to be a hypocrite and said so. This attitude did not conform to the teaching of the Savior. The Lord said that if discord existed between brethren, they should meet privately to solve their problems. If that method failed, then the complaining brother was advised to take with him two others from the church. If that effort failed, the offender should be brought before the entire assembly and, if necessary, excommunicated (see Matthew 18:15–17). Paul did not believe in postponing until tomorrow something which needed

214

immediate attention. Peter's conduct had affected all believers; the matter was being discussed throughout the city. He had caused the problem, and Paul believed he should answer for his folly. Unless this matter were settled, other people could follow Peter's example and the authority of the assemblies would be undermined.

Public Instability . . . *Demanding*

The intensity of Paul's argument may be measured by his other statement. "But though we, or an angel from heaven, preach any other gospel unto you than that which we have preached unto you, let him be accursed" (Galatians 1:8). God had entrusted to Paul a very special revelation and any person who contradicted the Word of the Almighty was not a friend of the Savior. To suggest such a thing concerning the man whom the Lord had used at Pentecost was a terrible indictment, but Paul was not a respector of persons. It is interesting to consider that Peter never issued a rebuttal. If he quietly accepted Paul's rebuke and refused to defend his foolish act, then he proved himself to be one of the greatest of all Christians. It is always wise to remember that Christians are not condemned because of their mistakes; God is more concerned with the manner in which they handle the situation. Even grave errors can be turned into stepping stones by which the fallen can reach higher heights of achievement.

Nevertheless, it should be remembered that the fundamental principles of the Gospel were only then being formulated; the course was being charted for generations to come. If all people were created equal in the sight of God, manmade laws should never be permitted to exploit underprivileged people. The leaders of the early church settled their differences with words; unfortunately, the modern world prefers to use guns!

40

PETER IS ACCOMPANIED BY HIS WIFE

"Have we not power to lead about a sister, a wife, as well as other apostles, and as the brethren of the Lord, and Cephas?" (1 Corinthians 9:5).

Simon Peter was indisputably a married man; there are theologians who believe he was the first pope of the Roman Catholic Church, but how they harmonize their doctrine of celibacy with his marital status is a problem which has never been explained. There is another difficulty which is even harder to understand. At the commencement of the Lord's ministry He entered the home of Peter and healed a mother-in-law (see Luke 4:38–39). Simon's wife was not mentioned again for a long period of time. Paul suggests that toward the end of Simon's ministry she became her husband's traveling companion, and ancient writings state that when she was about to die for her faith, Peter said: "Remember, my dear, the Lord." Where had she been in all those intervening years? Why was the lady not mentioned throughout Peter's ministry? That is a question which in all probability cannot be answered. Was she caring for her sick mother or had the first wife died, and Peter married a second time? It seems strange that for many years Simon Peter continued to serve the Lord actively but no reference was ever made regarding his wife.

However, she was mentioned (1 Corinthians 9:5) traveling with Peter and was used by Paul to support his claim to his apostolic authority. Apparently certain critics had complained about the wives of Christian leaders being permitted to accompany their husbands on church business. Some leaders were already requesting celibacy as a requisite for clergymen and others, perhaps because of the expense involved, were attempting to change a custom. The complications connected with that situation do not concern us, but the fact that Simon was accompanied by his spouse indicates she was helping in the work done by her partner. It must be concluded therefore that when Peter wrote his epistles and summed up his faith, he expressed also the faith of his partner. Blessed is the pastor whose wife lovingly supports her husband in extending the kingdom of God.

HOMILY NO. 10

Peter . . . *Who Fell In Love With A Word (1 Peter 1:19)*

It is sometimes surprising how a single word expresses great intensity of feeling. Many men and women who have been deeply stirred by outstanding events instinctively choose the strongest adjectives, and even then feel their utterances are inadequate. Simon Peter was a man of varying moods. He had known the mountaintops and also the valleys of human experience. Supreme joy had been followed by abject despair; yet through all the changing fortunes of his discipleship, he had known the constancy of his Lord's kindness. When Peter became an old man his sacred reminiscences were expressed in two epistles, and in both these letters he betrays his love for the word "precious."

The Precious Trials

When Paul wrote to the Romans he mentioned a very special fact: "And we know that all things work together for good to them that love God, to them who are the called according to his purpose" (Romans 8:28). Peter would have endorsed that statement, for throughout his career he had endured many trials and hardships. When in retrospect he reviewed everything, he realized each detail of his life had been woven into a glorious fabric depicting the faithfulness of his Lord. Therefore it was with certainty that he said to his friends: "The trial of your faith is much more precious than of gold" (1 Peter 1:7). The apostle assured his readers that out of the testings would emerge something to enrich them eternally. The scars suffered on earth would produce the brightest stars in their crown of life.

The Precious Blood of Christ

"Forasmuch as ye know that ye were not redeemed with corruptible things, as silver and gold . . . but with the precious blood of Christ, as of a lamb without blemish and without spot" (1 Peter 1:18, 19). Perhaps it is very fitting that this should represent Peter's use of the word. As an orthodox Jew he had been acquainted with the practice of offering a half-shekel of silver as atonement money for his soul. Peter now realized that the Old Testament types had been fulfilled in Christ; that redemption had been provided through the Lamb of God. It is worthy of consideration that nowhere in the Old Testament is the blood of the offering referred to as "the precious blood." Christ superseded all that had ever gone before.

The Precious Corner Stone

"Behold, I lay in Sion a chief corner stone, elect, precious: and he that believeth in him shall not be confounded. Unto you therefore which believe *he is precious*" (1 Peter 2:6–7). Peter recognized that the Gospel had changed everything. The importance of the priesthood of all believers far exceeded the Levitical order. Even the grandeur of the temple was now of little importance, for the fellowship of saints had created another dwelling in which true fellowship and worship would be preeminent. *Behind the corner stone* Peter found shelter from the storms of life. *In the corner stone* he found the strength that united and linked the other living stones of the spiritual temple. *Upon the corner stone* he found the confidence with which he and all others could rest in safety. Christ fully met the need of His Church. He was very precious!

The Precious Faith

"Simon Peter, a servant and an apostle of Jesus Christ, to them that have obtained like precious faith with us" (2 Peter 1:1). As Peter grew in grace he realized that the Gospel of Christ included much more than reconciliation to God. It was very wonderful to be brought nigh to God by the power of the Cross, but through the merits of the Savior the one-time enemy would be transformed into the likeness of God's Son. Grace and peace obtained through Christ at conversion could be *multiplied* through the soul's increasing knowledge of God and the Savior. In every conceivable way the new faith superseded the old one. The traditions of the fathers had been swept aside by the intimacy of this union with the Godhead. The Gospel was not for the privileged few, but for all the people in the world. It was indeed a precious faith.

The Precious Promises

"According as his divine power hath given unto us all things that pertain unto life and godliness, through the knowledge of Him that hath called us to glory and virtue: Whereby are given unto us *ex-*

ceeding great and precious promises" (2 Peter 1:3–4). Simon Peter could not foresee all the future details of his life, but he remained calm in the confidence that God's promises were true and faithful. They met every phase of human need. The Lord's promise, "I will never leave thee, nor forsake thee," was music for his soul; and every time he set out on a journey he recalled his Master's words, "Lo, I am with you alway." The promises of God were wonderful, and it was not really surprising that he described them as "exceeding great and precious."

The apostle was a great human and fully demonstrated the fact that the Spirit of God can lift a man above his failures in order to make him an instrument of blessing to countless thousands of people.

The Precious Savior

"Unto you therefore which believe he is precious" (1 Peter 2:7).

Simon Peter appreciated all that Christ had given to him. Grace for every trial; cleansing for every sin; shelter from every blast of life's tempests; promises for every emergency, and faith for all situations in life. Yet, in the final analysis, greater than all was the Lord Himself. Above and beyond any material or spiritual gift, the Savior was the brightest star in Peter's sky. As the bride in the Song of Solomon said: "He is altogether lovely" (Song of Solomon 5:16). Christ was the beloved Son of God; the King of angels; the Redeemer of a lost world; the joy of the past; the help of the present, and the hope for ages to come. He was the incomparable Jesus of Nazareth, the One Who for time and eternity would be worthy of praise. Mrs. Rhea F. Miller (1894–1966) expressed Simon Peter's faith when she wrote:

> I'd rather have Jesus than silver or gold:
> I'd rather be His than have riches untold:
> I'd rather have Jesus than houses or land,
> I'd rather be led by His nailed-pierced hand.
>
> He's fairer than lilies of rarest bloom,
> He's sweeter than honey from out the comb.
> He's all that my hungering spirit needs,
> I'd rather have Jesus and let Him lead.

219

Than to be the king of a vast domain;
Or be held in sin's dread sway.
I'd rather have Jesus than anything
This world affords today.

What Jesus Is

"To the artist, He is the one altogether lovely
  (Song of Solomon 5:15)
To the architect, He is the chief cornerstone (1 Peter 2:6)
To the astronomer, He is the sun of righteousness (Malachi 4:2)
To the baker, He is the bread of life (John 6:35)
To the banker, He is the hidden treasure (Matthew 13:44)
To the builder, He is the sure foundation (Isaiah 28:16)
To the carpenter, He is the door (John 10:7)
To the doctor, He is the great physician (Jeremiah 8:22)
To the educator, He is the great teacher (John 3:2)
To the engineer, He is the new and living way (Hebrews 10:20)
To the farmer, He is the sower and Lord of harvest (Luke 10:2)
To the florist, He is the rose of Sharon (Song of Solomon 2:1)
To the geologist, He is the rock of ages (1 Corinthians 10:4)
To the horticulturist, He is the true vine (John 15:1)
To the judge, He is the only righteous judge of man
  (2 Timothy 4:8)
To the juror, He is the faithful and true witness (Revelation 3:14)
To the jeweler, He is the pearl of great price (Matthew 13:46)
To the lawyer, He is counselor, lawgiver, and true advocate
  (Isaiah 9:6)
To the newspaper man, He is tidings of great joy (Luke 2:10)
To the oculist, He is the light of the eyes (Proverbs 29:13)
To the philanthropist, He is the unspeakable gift
  (2 Corinthians 9:15)
To the philosopher, He is the wisdom of God (1 Corinthians 1:24)
To the preacher, He is the Word of God (Revelation 19:13)
To the sculptor, He is the living stone (1 Peter 2:4)
To the servant, He is the good master (Matthew 23:8–10)
To the statesman, He is the desire of all nations (Haggai 2:7)
To the student, He is the incarnate truth (1 John 5:6)
To the theologian, He is the author and finisher of our faith
  (Hebrews 12:2)
To the toiler, He is the giver of rest (Matthew 11:28)

To the sinner, He is the Lamb of God Who takes the sin away
(John 1:29)
To the Christian, He is the Son of the Living God, the Savior, the
Redeemer, and the Loving Lord."

(Author Unknown. Copied from *One Hundred More Hymns Stories*, Kenneth W. Osbeck, Kregel Publications, Grand Rapids, Michigan.)

INDEX OF HOMILIES

BIBLIOGRAPHY

Barclay, William. *The Daily Study Bible*. Philadelphia: Westminster Press, 1976.

Matthew Henry's Commentary. London: Fleming Revell and Company, 1710.

Powell, Ivor. *Bible Highways*. Grand Rapids, Michigan: Kregel Publications, 1959.

Powell, Ivor. *Luke's Thrilling Gospel*. Grand Rapids, Michigan: Kregel Publications, 1965.

Powell, Ivor. *John's Wonderful Gospel*. Grand Rapids, Michigan: Kregel Publications, 1983.

Powell, Ivor. *Mark's Superb Gospel*. Grand Rapids, Michigan: Kregel Publications, 1985.

Powell, Ivor. *Bible Pinnacles*. Grand Rapids, Michigan: Kregel Publications, 1985.

Powell, Ivor. *Matthew's Majestic Gospel*. Grand Rapids, Michigan: Kregel Publications, 1986.

Powell, Ivor. *The Amazing Acts*. Grand Rapids, Michigan: Kregel Publications, 1991.

The Pulpit Commentary. Grand Rapids, Michigan: Wm. B. Eerdman Publishing Company, 1950.

Thayer, J. H. *The Greek English Lexicon*. Edinburgh: T. and T. Clark, 1958.

Thompson, W. M. *The Land and the Book*. London: Thomas Nelson and Company, 1910.

The Zondervan Pictorial Encyclopedia of the Bible. Grand Rapids, Michigan: Zondervan Publishing House, 1977.